Opening the Third Eye

A Collection of Teachings to Illuminate the Spirit

Vessa Rinehart-Phillips

Opening the Third Eye:
A Collection of Teachings to Illuminate the Spirit

First edition printed: Spring 2005
Second edition printed Spring 2006

Second Edition: ISBN: 1-891962-29-9
First Edition: ISBN: 1-891962-27-2

Published by:
Personal Transformation Press
8300 Rock Springs Road
Penryn, CA 95663
Phone: (916) 663-9178
Fax: (916) 663-0134

To order more copies of this book, please contact the publisher or the author at (858) 509-7582, or visit the author's websiteat www.myintuition.net

Edited and designed by Tony Stubbs (www.tjpublish.com)

Printed in the United States of America

Table of Contents

Acknowledgments

This book is dedicated to the members of the "Friends of Blanche" writers group—specifically Lisa Shapiro, Dr. Aileen Stanley, Dr. Gail Smith, Dr. Sonia Carbonell and of course, Blanche Maude Earl Pickett.

I also want to extend my gratitude to all those who helped me in my spiritual growth. I would not be where I am today without you.

And to my husband, Randy, for his never-ending patience and support.

Introduction

After years of working for a psychic institute in Northern California, I decided to start my own clairvoyant center in San Diego. Over two decades, I have taught psychic techniques to thousands of people and produced numerous CDs and tapes in order to help people further their own spiritual growth, read the aura, and enrich their lives.

At the request of several of my students, I decided to gather some of the teachings and clairvoyant philosophies in a book to help illuminate the journey for those who wish to find their own answers.

Many of the teachings in this book are also available on CD and through workshops, classes, and clinics. For a full list of products, see the back of the book.

I hope you enjoy *Opening the Third Eye.*

Chapter 1

Are You Using Your Intuition, Clairvoyance, and Accessing Your Psychic Abilities?

I BELIEVE THAT EVERYONE HAS some form of intuition, psychic ability, or clairvoyance—and I use these three words "intuition," "psychic," or "clairvoyance" interchangeably. Most people do not like to use the word "psychic" because it denotes an image of Madam Zorro with a turban on her head reading palms on a street corner telling you doomsday messages about your upcoming death. "Psychic" means so much more than that.

Using intuition can mean the difference between being in control of your life versus being influenced by other's thoughts unknowingly. It can be a way of being in control of your future. If you have been successful in business, chances are that you have used some of your spiritual abilities.

I also believe that most people do some form of reading. They look at their co-workers and can pick up whether or not they are having a good day. They "read" the thoughts of some of their children.

There are many ways to read. You can read from three areas of the body, meaning that you, the spirit, focus on the part of the body in which a chakra is located. You can read from the second chakra which is in your intestinal area. You might get a "gut feeling" about not going down a particular street. You might know who to sit next to or not sit next to on the bus. Or you may have a bad feeling about a job applicant and decide not to hire him. Reading from the second chakra is a powerful way to read. It's as if you have a built-in radar that detects energy, the safety of a situation and the feelings of others.

Another way to read is from the seventh chakra. The seventh chakra is at the top of your head. It is the chakra containing the information on knowing. Have you ever heard someone say, "I just knew it off the top of my head?" They hadn't read about it. They hadn't studied it in school. They just knew it. This means they are reading from the seventh chakra. If you have an inner knowing and you don't know how you came to that conclusion, then you are probably reading off the top of your head.

The best way to read is from the sixth chakra. Using the sixth chakra, you actually "see" the energy, rather than just know or feel that it is real. I teach my clairvoyant students to close their eyes to assist them in accessing the sixth chakra. In the psychic tools class, we teach a technique called "Running Your Energy," which helps the student to bring energy from the earth and the universe into the feet and the top of the head. The energy is then directed through the center of the head in order to stimulate the pineal gland. When the pineal gland is vibrating, it helps students to see the colors of energy with their eyes closed.

Sometimes you can stimulate your pineal gland without running energy. You can simply close your eyes, and imagine sitting in the center of your head behind your eyes, as if you were sitting in a chair in your head. Then ask yourself silently, "What is the brightest color in the aura of the person sitting next to me?" Let the first answer come to you. If you actually "see" the color in your head, then you are already using your pineal gland to catch a glimpse of energy.

Using your pineal gland to read clairvoyantly is not a new concept. A more invasive way is recorded in ancient Hindu literature, which mention a spiritual practice in which a hole was drilled in one's forehead in order to access the pineal gland. A stick or thin object was inserted into the opening. The pineal gland was then stimulated by lightly turning the device to get the pineal gland to function more effectively. Using spiritual tools is easier and far less painful!

I believe we are born with higher clairvoyance as children, but we, as children, start to "match" the adults around us. If the adults are not using their sixth chakra to see energy, then we children learn to turn this ability off. Imagine you were born in a society of all blind people. The blind people wouldn't realize any advantage of having sight since they don't have it themselves. Then eventually you might not use your eyes either. This is what happens to most of us in childhood.

We are entering into an age of spiritual awakening in which psychic ability no longer diminishes right after birth, but starts to affect us as we age. We all are getting glimpses of using our ability by having telepathy, precognition or a "gut feeling" about someone.

People are opening up to their intuition. If you'd mentioned chakras or that you teach people to read the aura to a person standing in line at the bank 25 years ago they would have thought you crazy and moved away from you as quickly as possible. Today, if you tell others that you teach people how to read the aura, they respond, "What color is mine?"

Chapter 2

What Is the Significance of Reincarnation and Past Lives in Your Current Life?

WHEN I WAS A CHILD, I had an invisible playmate. I thought I had imagined a leopard jogging along side of me as I ran along the canal in New Mexico where I grew up. Imagining that I was a man with this leopard, when I later ran track in physical education at my junior high in Texas, I continued "seeing my leopard" in my mind. At that time, I wasn't sure why, and even though I was a young female, while I ran or jogged, I would picture myself as a tall man.

When I turned 18, I went to see a psychic who immediately said, "You have a past life as a man in Africa with a pet leopard. In fact, the leopard is here with you now in spiritual form." I just about fell off my chair. How could this lady have known that?

"Why should a psychic look at past lives?" you might ask when thinking about getting a psychic reading. As a reader myself, I rarely look at past lives during a psychic reading unless the lives somehow pertain to what's going on for the seeker in this lifetime. Much of our current behavior can be traced back to past lives. Often, we bring the information from the past life forward to aid us in the current life.

You might envision your past lives as a bunch of files in a file cabinet. When you are ready to change careers, for example, you might open up this file cabinet and pull out all of the files where you made a successful career change. I've even seen people pull up past lives in which they weren't successful or they failed at a task in their past lives. Examining failure helps us avoid the same mistakes a second time.

The clairvoyant students in the six month program often read past lives at the free healing clinic. Explaining a certain behavior that an individual has can be the first step in changing that behavior. I knew a secretary who suddenly had a problem typing because her third finger on her right hand would uncontrollably start hitting the letter "k" every few strokes. It was greatly impacting her work because even the simplest memo was laced with k's. She came into the clinic and asked the clairvoyant reader to give her a healing. The reader saw that she had severed a finger in a previous life, and that lifetime had somehow been pulled forward and was impacting her life now. The reader helped to de-energize that life and re-file it into her past life aura. She immediately stopped having the problem at work.

When my friend John first joined the clairvoyant program, he resisted the idea of reading past lives because he didn't believe in them. He was brought up in Texas and he jovially boasted, "People from Texas don't have past lives!"

The director of the psychic institute insisted that he learn the technique to see a past lives. He reluctantly agreed and the first person he read was a neophyte lady who came in for a reading.

John used the past life reading method that was taught to him. He immediately saw, in his mind's eye, that she had used toothpicks in her lifetime as a cave woman, and that she had been in the same relationship with the man she was with now. John got the impression that they fought about the issue of toothpicks. He thought he was imagining things.

He wondered, *How could this be real?* He also thought this sounded ridiculous, but he found the courage to tell her about it anyway. To his surprise, the lady he was reading opened up her purse, which was filled with toothpicks.

"Thank you," she said. "I never knew why I always carry so many toothpicks with me and you have explained it to me. Now that I have the answer, I don't have to carry them anymore. I've had many fights with my husband over my strange desire to carry these toothpicks around."

During my 22 years of spiritual training, I've learned many things about life through reading past lives. For example, we live on a planet that has had intelligent life for thousands of years more than scientists and archeologists realize.

One of my students read a past life in a man where he was driving a vehicle, and the past life was thousands of years back. I believe from the past life readings that I've given that advanced cultures existed long before our scientists claim. Many articles appear in the newspapers every year about how scientists have found evidence of civilized societies, even human footprints embedded in volcanic rocks dating back millions of years ago. Tools and artifacts date back much further than modern day society acknowledges. Imagine a planet that was covered with lava several times over that would destroy most of the traces of earlier civilizations.

Another startling claim made by famous clairvoyants and prophets such as Edgar Cayce and by the Rosicrucian movement is that reincarnation was known and originally mentioned in the Bible, but that parts of the Bible have been left out.

There have been too many personal experiences for myself and observation by my students for me to believe that reincarnation isn't real. In a clairvoyant reading, often the seeker is having a relationship with someone who owed them in a past life.

To find some of your own answers, you can get a past life reading at a free reading clinic, or you can try reading yourself, by quieting yourself, closing your eyes and going within. Good questions to ask yourself while meditating are:

- What are you working out with members of your family—your mother, father, brother, or sister?
- Do you owe this person? Does he or she owe you?
- Is there something else going on that pertains to a past life that is affecting your relationship?

Listen to your inner voice for the answer. Awareness is the first step in change.

See you in this and the next lifetime!

Chapter 3

Who Controls Your Future? Are You Destined by Fate?

DID YOU EVER SEE THE movie *Groundhog Day*? In the movie, the lead character, Phil, played by Bill Murray, wakes up everyday and finds that everything is the same as the previous day. The people in the movie say the same things, the weather is the same, the circumstances are the same, and even the same song wakes him up on the radio. Being trapped in the same day again and again is a nightmare for Phil in the beginning of the story, and he has many bad days. He becomes depressed because nothing changes. Then he realizes that he can change his day to be a good day or a bad day depending on what he says, thinks and does. He starts to alter his day and learn new things. The audience sees a transformation in him where he starts to control his own future.

In many ways, this is a metaphor for life. When we are children, our parents, adults, and school teachers do many things for us and help us to shape our lives. We start to get the idea that other people or circumstances beyond our control are leading our lives. Another place we might pick up this behavior of passivity could be from watching hours and hours of television. We sit passively and say, "Okay, do it to me," rather than take an active role. It sometimes takes a while as an adult to outgrow this concept ... if we get there at all.

A good example of this is my friend Sarah who had grown up with parents who'd made her birthday special for her. When she was an adult, she still expected those around her to make her birthday extraordinary for her. If they did not do what she wanted, she became upset. She was angry at her boyfriend and friends for not giving to her in the way she wanted.

Then she had a revelation that *she* could make her day wonderful. On her 28th birthday, she decided to host her own party, inviting 80 people to her house, ordering two birthday cakes, hiring a live band and having plenty of food and drinks. She had an incredible time. Friends were able to give to her because she was giving to herself. They joined in on her happiness. They brought her presents and the day after her party, her boyfriend insisted on paying for all the expenses of the party. She had taken charge and created a special day for herself, instead of waiting for everyone else to do it.

I've heard people say, "I didn't do anything to create a new job or a relationship because if it doesn't just land in my lap, then it wasn't meant to happen." Many people today are very passive. They wait for things to happen to them, rather than go forth and create them. I challenge this way of thinking.

Life doesn't always just happen the way we want it to. We are on a freewill planet, meaning we have a path we follow, but we have freewill to change our path and opt on or off the direction of that path.

Sometimes I read people who ask me, "When am I going to get the _____ (relationship, career, weight—fill in the blank)?" But have they done anything to create it? Have they visualized it? Have they taken a course in a school to move in that direction? Have they told someone about it? Have they gone out to meet people? I saw a bumper sticker that said, "Expect a Miracle," but shouldn't it say, "Create a Miracle"?

Another factor that determines our fate is our thoughts. Thoughts are real and can merge in your aura or energy field. If you are a healer, you probably unconsciously absorb the beliefs and energy from others. Most of the time, we are not aware that the thoughts we think in our minds are not always our thoughts, but could be those of others. You can be controlled by someone else's thoughts once you accept them into your electromagnetic field.

Becoming a clairvoyant reader teaches you to become aware of the origin of the thoughts and concepts lodged in your aura that are controlling your actions, so that you can take the necessary steps to release them. The more awareness you have, the more freewill you can create to make educated choices. For example, if you don't know you are being controlled, then you can't change it. Awareness is the first step towards changing your life.

Your life is not random. It is created by you, and what you absorb into your aura. For a moment, pretend you are in charge of your life and that you are creating it, until it becomes real. Soon your energy will start to respond and you will be creating your life and your reality.

Taking an active role in creating your life is easier than you think. Start today by spending five minutes picturing the perfect day in your life when you first wake up and before you go to sleep. Your mind and energy want to create what you tell them. Having the thoughts and actions in place influences your direction in life.

Now—go create a nice day for yourself!

Chapter 4

Can You Recover from Disappointments Without Losing Your Enthusiasm for Life?

HAVING A BAD EXPERIENCE CAN sometimes leave a "picture" or stuck thought in your aura—the area two feet around your body. Thoughts are real and occupy space. When you leave a negative picture in your aura, it begins to attract energy.

Often, you then create experiences to validate that negative image. For example, let's say Bill sees a competitor taking his client. He becomes upset and creates a negative image in his mind that says, "Competitors take my clients!" He does not release the energetic charge on that thought. Thoughts can collect energy, so when Bill agonizes over the event with the competitor who took his client, his energy starts to go into the image. Because Bill is powerful, the image starts to manifest, grows, and becomes energized. Soon, Bill has many competitors taking his clients, thus validating the stuck energy pattern in his reality.

In the Psychic Tools Class, you learn to isolate the negative experience in the aura and de-energize it so you can recall the experience without having it manifest more of the undesired outcome. You no longer are controlled by the negative experience. Since you have removed an energetic "charge" on the thought, it does not collect energy.

Some gurus teach a mantra or an "erasure" technique. Erasing the experience serves as an immediate relief from being stuck on a thought or concept. Using a mantra or erasure takes out the memory of the bad experience. In Bill's case, he will completely forget the experience of the competitor taking his client.

Using a mantra or erasure might seem like a great solution, but if you consider that we humans incarnate here on planet Earth to gain life experience, erasing all memories is not a great solution. I have learned that it is not productive to erase all your pictures or thoughts because you, the spirit, learn through experience, and when you erase all your thoughts and memories, you must then recreate them all over again. There was a reason you acquired that life experience in the first place.

Some spiritual teachers teach another way to deal with disappointing experiences—to leave the body in order to avoid negative and painful experiences. Visualizing yourself away in another world is a way of leaving the body. This is not the answer either because the negative energy and negative prints are stored in your body while you are not there. Negativity stuck in your aura and body eventually manifests into some sort of problem, unhappiness or disease.

Learning to de-energize pictures or negative thoughts using psychic tools releases the charge of the negativity in the thought, but you still retain the memory of the experience. The clairvoyant training program teaches several ways to de-energize pictures, along with tools to increase your awareness, work with energy, and start to find your own answers. De-energizing the experience allows you to remember the experiences you have been through, but it does not allow them to take away your happiness even if it was a negative experience.

Here's another example. Say you broke up with your boyfriend, and now you want him back, but he's moved on to someone else. You keep thinking about him again and again. You can collect images of him into an energetic rose, just by imagining the rose out in front of you absorbing thoughts and colors that remind you of him. Once you get a sense that the rose is full of the past thoughts, you can imagine that it bursts or explodes into a billion pieces and disintegrates. Congratulations, you have just freed yourself from stuck thoughts. There might be thousands of strongly charged images of him in your aura. It might take exploding several roses full of thoughts until you completely feel you are not controlled by the obsession of your ex-boyfriend, but know that relief will be yours soon.

Chapter 5

Can't You Just Learn to Read an Aura and Access Your Clairvoyant Abilities by Reading a Book, Alone by Yourself?

INTUITIVE DEVELOPMENT CLASSES AT INTUITIVE Insights are set up so you learn two or three spiritual or psychic tools weekly to use in your life. You practice these tools with other students in the class in a safe environment, and then you go out into the "unreal" world to apply them during the next few days. When you come back the following week, you learn more techniques in addition to reviewing what you learned during the previous week.

Repetition of psychic tools is important because you are retraining yourself in how to think and use your energy. You also need the classroom setting to have the opportunity to practice and work with others in a safe environment, free from invalidation.

The saying, "practice makes perfect" is also true for spiritual tools.

A student, Lisa, who attended the clairvoyant class, learned the tool of grounding. The next day, she attended her brother's graduation which was held on a football field at his school. When the ceremony was over, the crowd sitting in the bleachers immediately rushed onto the football field. Lisa and her family wanted to find her brother so they could take him out to lunch. Her family said, "How are we going to find him in the midst of all those thousands of people?"

Lisa thought, "I'll ground myself to the planet, and I'll ground my brother. This way, we'll be the only two people who are grounded at this event." After she grounded herself and her brother, she walked into the crowd and instantly found him.

Another student, Carol, was having severe financial problems. She took the Psychic Tools class and learned the tool of using an energetic rose. She pictured an energetic red rose in front of her and decided to use this spiritual tool to help her in a materialistic way. She put the rose up in front of her with the intention that it would help her find some money. She even whispered, "Rose, lead me to abundance." As she walked along the street, she suddenly got a feeling that the rose was veering to the right of her, a few feet off into a side street. She followed the rose and walked down the side street. She looked down at the sidewalk and found $80 folded up and lying on the street. She picked it up and resumed her original route home.

When Carol arrived home, she opened her cabinet to see what she could make for dinner. She found she had two choices: macaroni and cheese or spaghetti. She again became aware of the rose guiding her to choose the tomato sauce and to have spaghetti.

She picked up the can of paste and opened it with a can opener. When she pulled back the lid, written on the other side was, "Congratulations, you have won $5." She was able to practice using her psychic tools to create for herself.

Sure, you could read a book and finish with it within a few hours, but if you do not use and practice the information you have learned, it is the same as if you never attained the information in the first place.

The past 18 years of teaching clairvoyance have shown me when the student is ready, the teacher will appear. Many times, people driving through the area drop in to get a reading at the free clinic, and end up staying for eleven months to complete the beginning and advanced Clairvoyant Training Programs.

In the same way that I endorse having a spiritual teacher, I also believe that you should not have your teacher become a guru to you, to the point where you cannot find your own answers.

"The answers are within," says the Bible. Jesus appeared as a spiritual teacher and enlightened millions to the presence of God, so that each of us could communicate directly with the divine. Jesus' mission was not to make people dependent on him for information. "Behold I send you out as sheep in the midst of wolves," and, "The works that I do and greater can you do."

Okay, I'll get off my soap box now!

Chapter 6

Why Did the One Thing You Really Wanted in Life Slip Through Your Fingers?

AN EXCEPTIONALLY ATTRACTIVE LADY, ABOUT 34 years old, came in for a clairvoyant reading from me about two months ago. She was crying and claiming that she was suicidal. The reason? The man she loved had told her he was not going to be with her anymore. Emily (not her real name) was devastated. "How can he do this? There's nothing left to live for," she cried. "Why is this happening? Why did God do this to me?"

With my eyes closed, I saw, in my mind's eye, swirls of red energy around her head, which was the energy she was releasing and the color of her anguish. When a color appears in my mind, I ask myself, or my inner voice, the meaning of each color I see. Then I receive a silent answer within. This shade of red meant distress.

When you read clairvoyantly, you sit across from someone and find answers about the seeker inside of yourself. "The answers lie within," says the Bible, and that's exactly how to be a good reader—go within yourself. Silently and telepathically, I asked Emily's higher self the same questions she had asked me, and I heard a clear answer inside my head.

I opened my eyes and gave Emily my answer, "Your higher self is showing me that you have spent a lifetime of putting people, objects, and money before your soul, and now you are being asked to find and rediscover yourself again as an individual. You are looking outside yourself rather than listening to your voice within. This happened to you as a wake-up call, to act as a catalyst to get you to realize that you are not your thoughts, your pictures, ideas, or relationships, but instead you are a spirit who creates experiences from which to learn and grow."

Emily realized that this was true and started to see the big picture that she was not her creations, but rather was learning and growing from her experiences.

I have seen many people experience wake-up calls to get them to turn inward towards their inner voice. There is a reference to this phenomenon in several famous spiritual teachings, including the Bible: "What if a man gained the whole world and lost his own soul?" asks Jesus. If you gain the whole world and lose yourself in the process, the universe assists you in finding yourself again. Instead of thinking that this is the end, think of it as a reminder to refocus on yourself and listen to yourself.

I knew a man, Robert (not his real name), and his business partner who scraped together a down payment to purchase a million-dollar commercial fishing boat for a moneymaking venture. It was going to be hard work at first, but in a few years, each planned to start living the high life. After owning the boat a few days but before it had been properly insured, it was stolen. Robert and his partner now owed the bank a million dollars—which was money they did not have. Adding to the tragedy, Robert's business partner immediately fled the country and was never heard from again. Robert was plagued with depression, trying to make ends meet and pay back the million dollar judgment on a menial salary. Soon afterwards, he was diagnosed with cancer. Spiritually he had decided to die since he saw no way out of the dilemma.

Robert came in for a series of readings and the readers were able to energetically heal the destructive experiences and see that there was hope. In his aura, one of the readers saw that there was an accountant who could help him lift his financial burden from the judgment and get a new life. Robert sought out and found the accountant. Together they negotiated a small settlement with the bank. Robert started to feel better and hence his cancer instantaneously stopped progressing and began to regress, then disappeared.

When Robert received a healing, it changed his spiritual path so he could learn the lesson he chose to learn and could then move on to the next lesson in life. When you receive your wake-up call, be positive, and go within. Ask yourself, "What do I need to change in my life?" and imagine the best things will happen for you.

This is not the end, but the beginning of you knowing yourself.

Chapter 7

Are You Really Doomed to Die Because of "Bad" Genes?

SO YOUR RELATIVE HAS HEART disease, diabetes, cancer, etc. And now your doctor is putting the "fear of God" into you to get checked and checked—annually, semi-annually, and quarterly for this hereditary disease. But are you *really* doomed because someone in your family has contracted a disease?

Headlines in newspapers speak of people having genetic predispositions to diseases, which causes great fear amongst the masses. Even some doctors who haven't completely studied the genetic research are provoking paranoia amongst society. This fear creates a victim cycle in which people feel that they have no power over disease. We are now a society that lives in fear of sickness. And everyone seems to be affected, because inevitably, there is someone, perhaps a distant relative in your family, who is struggling with an ailment.

Let's examine the above concepts: It is true, research has found genes that generally make someone more susceptible to diseases, but are we looking at this from a spiritual perspective or from an atheistic, non-spiritual point of view?

The atheistic point of view says, "You can't change. You're doomed to bad genes. If you have the fatal disease gene, then there is a 100% chance of your early death." When society, your friends, co-workers and even yourself perpetuate this energy, you are stuck in the energy and thoughts of fear which, I believe, can contribute to disease.

This leads to people having radical medical procedures or taking medications to prevent this so-called destiny from happening. In the case of breast cancer, some women in the United States have even removed their breasts because someone in the family had breast cancer, even though the woman shows no signs. In my opinion, this is ridiculous … and a result of the power of hysteria.

I recently asked a middle-aged man, "What do you plan to do when you retire?"

He answered, "Well, my wife will probably die soon, so I think I might move to a foreign country and become a missionary."

I asked, "Is your wife sick?"

"Oh, no. She's healthy," he answered. "It's just that she has two relatives who died of cancer, so she'll probably get it and die, too."

I thought, it's a sad time we live in that instead of using the new medical research to help us with our lives, we instead doom our loved ones, and live in fear ourselves of dying from "genetic" diseases.

Let's take a look at the genetic predisposition of acquiring breast cancer. Hereditary breast cancers account for only 10% of the annual incidence of breast cancer in the United States, and the two main genes responsible for this susceptibility are BRCA1 and BRCA2. That means that 90% of breast cancer is *not* genetic, but instead are *lifestyle* related. It also turns out that researchers have found that, even if you fall in the 10% category that has the cancer genes, the chance that you will get breast cancer in your lifetime is below 60% depending on your lifestyle habits, so there's no reason to do radical medical procedures. Instead, *change your lifestyle.*

Similar findings are being reported about prostate cancer in men. An article about prostate cancer from the Prostate Cancer Helpline states: "When people have migrated from Japan to the USA in the past, the rate of prostate cancer in their descendants has risen greatly. Since their genetic make-up is largely similar, as they have married within their own ethnic communities, the new risk of prostate cancer is likely to be related to environmental factors. Diet is an important one of these. Another pointer to reinforce this conclusion is that the levels of cancer in the East are rising. This coincides with changes in lifestyle – more people are living Western lifestyles and eating Western style foods."

In the advanced psychic training classes, clairvoyant students work on healing their genetic make-up, keeping the best, and removing the worst. They reprogram the energy of the cells and body disposition to affect their so-called "destiny." Thoughts are real and energy is real. If you think a thought, your energy goes through the idea and then starts to create it. It doesn't matter if the thought is positive or negative. And if you think a negative thought about your body falling victim to a terminal illness, that vibration permeates your cells. And the cells, just like your energy, want to respond. One way to combat this is, whenever you have a negative thought about your body, immediately imagine that thought as a color and imagine that color being pulled out of you by gravity. Then replace that image with an extremely positive image of, say, you jogging on the beach in great health.

Thoughts can be hereditary, too. If you are around a negative thinker as a child, often you pick up that pattern of thinking. You might have learned to think and act just like your mother or father. It takes much effort as an adult to change patterns of thinking. The first step is to recognize that you *do* think in this way, just like your mother or grandmother or father. Next, imagine breaking up the pattern by releasing the colors out of your aura, just as you would release a depressing thought. You can change the way you think and act to bring forth a different outcome to your life.

Energy is not finite, nor is spirit unchangeable. The body, too, can radically change just from you changing your thoughts, your eating and exercise habits, as well as your routine, so you can become healthy and vibrant. I have even seen people overcome terminal illness by receiving a spiritual healing. In most cases, I believe that there is a spiritual cause that contributes to the illness. If you remove the spiritual cause, then the spirit begins to heal the body.

Another way I have seen people radically reverse any disease is by changing their diet. We in the United States don't eat well or know how to eat. We have high-fat, low fiber diets that are enzyme deficient. It's time we learned how to eat to contribute to superior health.

You are not doomed. Don't give in to the fear and hype of the media saying that you cannot alter your physical fate. Start by changing your thoughts and your energy by using psychic tools. Release the fear and the genetic energies out of your electromagnetic field—your aura and body—and heal yourself. Then radically change your diet, your daily routine, and your exercise schedule. Make the necessary changes today and live a lengthy, positive, productive existence.

Now, go live a long life!

Chapter 8

Does Being a Good Person Pay Off?

THE DICTIONARY DEFINES "KARMA" AS: "The total result of a person's actions and conduct during the successive phases of the person's existence, which in turn determines the person's destiny, outcome, or fate." Put more simply, you might say that what you exude into the world will come back to you next lifetime.

Over the past few years, we have been in the Age of Truth, meaning that everything that was hidden got uncovered and discovered . . . and sex, financial, and religious scandals headline our newspapers.

Now another interesting shift in the world's vibration has given yield to the Age of *Instant* Karma. Suddenly the energy you put out into the world is coming back to you sooner. No longer are we in an age where karma comes back next lifetime; karma is coming back to you now, this lifetime, and sometimes as quickly as a few weeks or months, or even in the same day.

Mary (not her real name) stole small items in stores, even though she had more than enough money to pay for the items since she and her husband owned a successful business. One day, Mary's house got robbed and many valuable possessions were stolen from her. Some of her employees also stole from her. This is an example of instant karma.

Working out your issues while you are in the body is more important than ever. People on their deathbeds try to rectify any former negative communications with loved ones because it is much easier to work out issues *while* you have the body, not after the body has died.

In the clairvoyant class, students practice communicating with the other side of the veil, with people who have died. Many of these spirits have shown us that it is much easier to work through stuck issues, thoughts, and communications while in the body, and not to wait until afterwards.

Practicing forgiveness for yourself and others is imperative. This does not mean that you have to allow someone to take advantage of you a second time. It merely means that you let go of the stuck energy in your aura and consciousness, so you do not take the hostility with you to the grave.

"What is bound on Earth is also bound in Heaven," admonishes the Bible. One might rephrase that, "What you haven't gotten over while you were alive in the body will still be an issue when you pass away."

You don't have to re-live and re-confront every episode. Perhaps you will never get another chance of changing the relationship with a person you transgressed against previously because you will never see him or her again. You can show kindness to the world by helping another individual or living being. I have watched people turn around their karmic fate by sending out the energy of compassion, joy, love, and peace, even if it is not to the same person against whom they have trespassed.

I know a man who killed many animals as a pre-teen and teenager. Later in life as an adult, he had the opportunity to change his karma by caring for a dog. He deeply regretted what he had done as a youth, but he remedied some of that by expressing love when he was older.

You can release your karma by working with three-dimensional energy as taught in the clairvoyant training program, or you can start immediately by saying, "I forgive myself for my wrongdoings and I forgive those around me for their wrongdoings against me." With this intention, you start to let go of the karma.

Start today, change your actions, and alter your destiny by becoming karma free.

Chapter 9

How to Live in a Fear-Based Society

RECENTLY A GUEST TEACHER, Shelley Hodgen, taught a class called: "Everything You Wanted to Know about Fear." In the workshop, Shelley asked students to write down all of their worst fears. The listed fears ranged from fear of losing everything, fear of bugs, fear of failure, fear of financial ruin, fear of death, and more.

While this was going on, in my mind's eye, I saw a white energy filling the room. Silently I asked my inner voice what this white energy was, and was told that it was the students' resistance to their fears. As people listed their most awful worries on a piece of paper, the energy of powerlessness began to get released. When people admitted and acknowledged their fears, it helped to stop the cycle of resistance from growing. As a clairvoyant, I could see that some of these fears were based on past life experiences and some were fears from childhood.

The general theme of the fears was that you, the spirit occupying the body, would not be in control and that someone or something outside your control would take over, rendering you powerless.

Resistance to these fears could cause some of them to be manifested. The way the resistance works is, if you resist something enough, you lock the energy into that thought. The non-movement of energy in your aura aids in creating the very situation you wish to avoid.

The first step to changing an energy pattern is to become aware of it. If you are not conscious of your fears, then how can you know what to work on in liberating yourself from them?

Once you acknowledge a fear, imagine releasing that fear with a grounding cord. A grounding cord is a three-dimensional visualization in which you access the gravitational pull of the planet to assist you in letting go of unwanted thoughts into the earth. Thoughts can stick in your consciousness and the energy field around your body. Imagine the thoughts of fear draining out of your body and subconscious mind, as if they were specks of dirt falling out of you to the center of the earth. At the center of the gravitational field, energy gets neutralized.

Releasing these images of fear also de-energizes the negative event for your mind, thus preventing these pictures from controlling you.

Replace the negative thoughts with a positive visualization of the best possible scenario. For example, if you are afraid of failing, see yourself succeeding. If you are afraid of drowning, see yourself swimming strongly and safely to the shore. See the thought in your mind's eye. Change the path of your energy into a positive one. If you work with energy and remove negative thoughts in your consciousness, then there is really nothing to be afraid of!

Chapter 10

The Energy of Completing Relationships

RECENTLY A GUEST TEACHER, David Pearce, spoke about, "The Energy of Completing Relationships." He led students through a step-by-step process on how to let go of a relationship, release the past, and embrace the future.

Sometime in your lifetime, you will probably end an important personal relationship, or perhaps you already left a job that you had for years, and after you left, you realized that you had all of your energy tied up in that one activity or person. Energy is not good or bad, but rather, it is either yours or someone else's.

We, as spirits, start to put our energy into a job or to another person, and when the relationship or job is over, we experience a loss, not only of the day-to-day communication, but a loss of our energy in our auras—the space around us.

I recently gave a clairvoyant reading to a woman who left her job after sixteen years. Even though she knew leaving was the healthiest thing for her and that she would eventually find another job, every day she went back in her mind to the relationship with the company, to the point where she could hardly function in her daily life. For many months, she even dreamed she was back at the old job. She had put so much energy into making the company work that it had become her identity. She received a healing, then purchased a tape on completing relationships and began to reclaim her energy from the previous employer. She then created a fabulous new job with more money, space, and validation ... and she became happier.

In a personal relationship, we create pictures, which are thoughts, of the other person. These thoughts stick in our bodies and the layers of the aura. The deposited thoughts and pictures of the other person collect on the edge of our aura. "You're the best person in the world," or, "You're so generous." These thoughts enter into our subconscious, and we start to believe these pictures and ideas until they become part of us.

Collecting positive thoughts on the edge of your aura is wonderful while everything is going well in the relationship, but what if the relationship ends and the thoughts from the other person are negative, as in, "You're the worst person in the world," or, "You're stingy." We then start to allow some of the negative thoughts to enter our consciousness and lower our self-esteem, which slows us down from creating our lives as quickly as we had been doing before.

In a long term relationship, we also start to adjust ourselves and our thought patterns to match those around us. We become programmed or conditioned to act in a specific manner. With negative images in your aura, you might start to act negatively. With positive images in the aura, you might start to act positively.

With psychic tools, you can begin to undo this type of conditioning after you end a relationship. It is important to release the negative images, so you can create your future. Also, it is important to release any energy—whether positive or negative—that you absorbed from the other person, because holding that energy in your body and aura serves as a doorway for that person's energy to come back into your space.

Another important step in making energetic separations from a partner is to free your energy that is stuck in goals you made for each other and plans you made together. This helps you create new opportunities for yourself. Perhaps you or your partner thought, "Let's get rich together!" Now that the relationship is over, you can call back your goal so you can manifest that aspiration with someone else.

Many times during a break-up, you may be in a vengeful mood and say, "I hope you never meet anyone else as nice as me." In wishing that, you leave your energy inside of your ex-partner and now you have karma with him or her. It's time to gather your energy—whether it is in the form of negative or positive thoughts, so you can use that energy for something else in life. Your energy cannot work for you if it is not in your possession.

Collecting these thoughts and pictures, and then releasing them, will aid in expediting the completion of the relationship and help you move on to something better.

Chapter 11

Why Do I Have This Problem?

WE GROW AND LEARN SPIRITUALLY by creating and solving problems. Some of the problems mirror what happened to us in our childhood. I knew a man who had been beaten up by his siblings as a child. As an adult, he was now being beaten up by the residents' association where he lived.

I also believe that people will recreate the same problem in order to learn a lesson, but do not always learn the lesson from the problems they are experiencing, so they unconsciously recreate the same problem again and again. I knew a woman who was a good driver, but her car got rear-ended three times in one month. She sometimes felt ignored by her husband, who was an attorney. As a child, she got attention from her father whenever she created a problem that he had to help her solve. She created the accidents to get attention from her husband. She came to the healing clinic and received a reading, in which she realized why she had been hit three times. She was then able to release the past and move forward. She has not had a car accident since her visit to the clinic.

Part of the magic of using psychic tools and getting a reading is that you can start to see how your current situation matches your childhood or previous circumstances. Once you identify the similarity, you can then end the cycle of this problem and move on in your growth. Sometimes you do not even have to know how the situation matches a previous one but can just release it.

One time, a lady in the clairvoyant training program decided to consciously create a problem, rather than having problems come to her. She grew up in an environment of lack, where she could have only half of anything given to her since she had to share it with others. She decided to create and envision the problem of having two of everything. So within a week, she had two relationships, two places to live, two phone bills and more. She quickly decided to go back to having one of everything. She felt that she had recovered from the events of her childhood. She demonstrated to herself that she could create and then solve problems of her choosing.

Take a moment and examine the problems you are solving in your life. Explore how the feelings of these current problems match previous feelings you had in the past. If you sense that you have learned this lesson, perhaps it's time for a healing and a reading so you can end the cycle of this problem and move on.

Chapter 12

Relationships: Can't We Just Get Along?

WE ARE IN THE ERA of finding growth through relationships. We are learning to get along with our lover, our parents, children, friends, co-workers, God, the IRS, and even our pets. Much of one's spiritual growth comes from relating to others.

True, you cannot force someone to love you or even to be reasonable, but you can connect to your higher self and do the best you can, relating to the world with the highest integrity and your greatest truth.

If you are unkind, creating destruction towards another, or lashing out at someone, you are not acting out of the higher part of your soul, and you are *creating* karma rather than *releasing* it. By creating ill will in the world, you create karma and postpone your growth until another time. If I may repeat that universal truth in the Bible, "What is bound on Earth is also bound in Heaven," means that if you have not worked it out through your physical actions, then you have not worked it out spiritually, either. You will *have* to work it out after you die. You can just as easily move spiritually backwards on your path, as move forward.

I knew a man who created much sadness in people's lives while he was alive. After he died, he visited me as a spirit and expressed how difficult it had been initially when he passed over because he experienced the pain he caused in other's lives. He eventually forgave himself, healed himself, and moved towards his own divinity. He showed me that if you work on your end of the relationship with someone, then you are free from going through the pain after you leave the body.

Relationships can be painful. Rejection, invalidation and fear can result from being in a relationship, which is why many people want to avoid them, preferring to live their life alone on a mountain top away from society. On the other hand, relationships with others can bring euphoria and incredible joy. Having relationships with people also is a way to accelerate your spiritual growth and awareness, because you are constantly processing what others bring to the world. You speed up the thoughts you are dealing with by dealing with more than just yourself.

Having a sense of yourself, your space, or your own essence, while being with others, is important. If you lose yourself in others, then you are not operating out of the highest part of yourself. Balancing your inner soul while relating to others is one of the ultimate purposes of human existence.

One way to do this is by learning spiritual or psychic tools to de-energize current thoughts that cause you to act out of character or your own essence. By learning to clairvoyantly read people, students find out what their own blocks are, and get to know themselves better, thus discovering their true essence.

They begin to have a better relationship with themselves. Having a good relationship and being comfortable with yourself allows for you to have better relationships with others.

Chapter 13

How Do You Handle Pain?

MOST EVERYONE KNOWS WHAT IT is like to touch a stove, burn yourself, and feel physical pain, but do you know how to handle spiritual and emotional pain? Some specific examples of spiritual and emotion pain are when someone rejects you, doesn't like you, doesn't approve of you, or doesn't like what you create. Or the people you admired as a child didn't have time for you and didn't want you around.

Sometimes spiritual and emotional pain are often far worse types of pain. For one, spiritual and emotional pain last much longer than physical pain. You might have the pain from these experiences with you for years, whereas the physical pain eventually subsides.

People use many different ways to escape from spiritual and emotional pain, since you can't just take an aspirin. I've seen instances where people will turn to other ways of numbing themselves in order not to have to see the pain. Watching hours and hours of television is an escape. Doing drugs, alcohol, being on the computer for excessive lengths of time, distractions of any sort, all take you out of the present situation. If the stored-up pain is great, it causes you, the spirit, to leave the body. This is what's referred to as an out-of-body experience.

There are many types of out-of-body experiences. One out-of-body experience is where you have your attention on an event in the future or the past. You actually send a part of yourself there, thus dividing yourself as a spirit. We think of an out-of-body experience as a strange psychic phenomenon, but in actuality, we have out-of-body experiences daily. We drive down the freeway focusing on our destination and only part of ourselves is driving the car. We sometimes operate our bodies on automatic when we are preoccupied and split, as a spirit. Have you ever driven to a destination, and once you arrive, realize that you didn't remember driving there?

People ask me, "How can I have an out-of-body experience?" I am amused by this question, because I am attempting to have an "IN-Body" experience, meaning that I want to stay present and clear to enjoy life, and process pain as it comes up using spiritual techniques.

When I give a clairvoyant reading, I see these stored-up pockets of pain having a great effect on the seeker. When you have a painful experience that you don't want to face, you store it in the body and the aura, and you, the spirit, take off. You lose some of your clarity and awareness. Sometimes emotional and spiritual pain can affect the memory banks, as you block out your experiences.

In the aura, these painful experiences are reflected as dull or dark colors. Enthusiasm or joy is reflected as bright or pastel colors. I see stored-up pain as pockets of red and black scattered through the energy field. These colors are often a reflection of the pain people have deposited in their conscious or subconscious mind.

Rather than storing pain, you can process it out of your aura or your body. Exercise, meditation, and using psychic tools are ways to process it out. When you learn to ground, run your energy, and release images, you start to process pain in a different way. You de-energize it and stay in-the-body, or, in other words, you stay clear, focused and in present time.

You can learn to read auras and in your spiritual development, learn to release stored pain. You can also retrain yourself in how to think and manage energy so you process out the pain instead of leaving your body. You then become more in-tune with yourself, happier, and more present.

Chapter 14

Is It Better To Be Serious or Amused?

CREATING THE MUSIC OF YOUR soul begins with mastering your "emotional piano scale." You can set your energy with the intention of vibrating at a particular key. In doing so, your energy will follow your intention, elevating the rest of your consciousness. In other words, if you want to be happy, pretend you are happy, and your psyche will follow shortly.

The complete frequency range of the emotional piano scale progresses down from joy to enthusiasm, amusement, neutrality, anger, apathy, and boredom. The bottom end of the scale moves from grief all the way to death.

The magic of human existence is in enthusiasm, in which all obstacles can be overcome. Exercising our enthusiasm motivates us to get over whatever obstacles there are. Emotionally healthy children have inherent exuberance and enthusiasm. The Bible says, "To enter into the kingdom of Heaven, come as a little child." So when you demonstrate enthusiasm, you are naturally becoming more spiritual and closer to Heaven on Earth.

When you are at the very top of the emotional range, you often will experience joy—the space where you see the positive in life and feel the harmony it brings. It is an overall sensation that you are just joyous and don't necessarily need a reason to have joy; you just are "in joy." Animals, too, can experience joy. Last week, some birds were playing in the sprinkler out in the yard, singing and swooping in a joyous manner. Their play served no purpose other than play.

Amusement is a spiritual tool of thinking that life is funny. A sense of humor can save you from a horrendous emotional downfall. If you are able to laugh at yourself, then you are able to separate from your thoughts and creations to realize that what you think and what you create are not you, the spirit. Laughter changes the magnetic charge in the aura, so pain or punishment bounces off your energy field. For example, if an adversary is angry at you, and you are simply amused about it, then his anger cannot control you.

Neutrality is seeing both sides of a dichotomy. It is different from apathy, because with neutrality there is no judgment, and you understand both sides. You have the power to see viewpoints but not take a side. A psychic reader trained to use neutrality in his spiritual counseling can read without judgment why a person is creating her life in a certain way. In saying hello to the soul, a reader can suddenly understand why the seeker has chosen that path.

Anger is a higher energy vibration than boredom or grief, because anger can be a motivation. When you are angry, the anger can move the stuck energy and thoughts stored in the aura. You then leave apathy, boredom and grief behind.

On this emotional scale, death is defined as no movement. The effortless growth of the aura ceases, and no new thoughts come into the mind. The colors of the energy field become dark, and the spirit leaves the body.

So, where do you want to be on the emotional piano scale? The world is waiting for your song.

Chapter 15

Spirituality versus Materialism: Can You Copy the Energy of the Rich and Become Wealthy?

AT ONE TIME, I was downright poor, living on a food allowance of $8 per week, but now my business and professional career are thriving, I started to think about how my previously dismal situation had changed to a life of prosperity.

After receiving my certification as a clairvoyant, healer and a member of the clergy in a metaphysical non-denominational Christian church in the San Francisco Bay Area, I found that many of the hundreds of students I served and ministered to lived below the poverty line. Possessions as basic as a car, a safe residence, or being out of debt, were difficult for these spiritual people.

In my spiritual training, I learned some life-changing universal truths. I started to know myself more than I thought was possible, and I mastered techniques to apply psychic tools to help govern my own life. Some of the concepts I studied were methods to protect myself from picking up energy and thoughts from others and how to keep my own life force around me. I also learned how to protect myself psychically from others. I explored how to read people and know what ideas were stored in their auras—the two-foot space around them encompassing their bodies.

One day as I counseled a penniless member of the church who told me that he was about to file bankruptcy, I pondered the questions, "Why are so many of these spiritual people poor?"

I offered a clairvoyant reading to as many people as I could, viewing their ability to create what they wanted. I gave free sessions to anyone who wanted spiritual insight to his or her prosperity. The metaphysical center attracted many different types of people, and I had dozens of people come to me—from the impoverished to the multimillionaire—and I began to see the energetic differences between the two groups of members. I narrowed down and categorized the differences between the rich and poor into seven categories. I soon found that if I, myself, copied the words, behaviors, and energy traits of the rich, good things started happening to me, including an increase in my own abundance, and in addition, money flowed toward me. When I felt that I had found the answers, I narrowed them down into seven secrets to yield what the universe had to offer. Now I'm able to teach my clairvoyant students ways to increase their prosperity and copy the energy of the rich to become rich, as well as have prosperity for myself.

Imagine merely replicating the energy and thought patterns of an affluent person and becoming rich yourself. Matching another's energy is easier than you can imagine, because life force energy is neutral and will create anything that the mind focuses on. In the Abundance and Prosperity workshops, countless people have turned their lives around from an existence of desperation to having a plethora of good fortune. By practicing clairvoyant tools, changing the way you think, and putting the concepts into practice, your life will change, too.

Now, let's explore one of the seven main secrets, then put that into effect, so you can alter your thoughts, energy, and outcome of your creations. The rest of the secrets are written in my book, *Why the Rich Are Rich.*

When I give a clairvoyant reading, the number one difference I see between a person who has abundance and a poor person is that an abundant person has the ability to form a picture—a detailed picture, in his mind of whatever he desires. Rich people can see an image, focus on it long enough for their energy to go through the mental photograph, and manifest it. This may sound too basic and simple, but there are millions of people who do not have the correct thought process to get rich—namely by holding a positive image in the mind long enough for energy to go through it.

For example, Joseph Strauss, the man who built the Golden Gate Bridge, pictured every part of the bridge—the nuts and bolts, and the way it would work—long before the blueprints were drawn. Once the blueprints, mock-ups, and funding were there, the construction began. Strauss had the whole picture in his head before he started the process.

Your life force energy is extremely powerful. Energy has the same characteristics as a ray of light passing through a filter that manifests the outcome, similar to an overhead projector that illuminates a crisp transparency. The sharper the image that the beam passes through, the clearer the projection. The thoughts in your mind act as your filters, so if your thoughts are distinct, then the end product is also specific.

ENERGY >>> THOUGHT >>> OUTCOME

Society has taught us that thoughts happen and then disappear, but in truth, thoughts are real things occupying space. Thoughts can live in a site, stay in a room, in one's aura, or on a street corner. Have you ever known of a restaurant that failed, and then any new companies in the same location also went out of business even though the eatery across the street succeeded? This phenomenon occurs because the spiritual vibration and mental picture of failure held by the previous occupants still inhabit that locale.

Many times during my career as a clairvoyant, I have provided a service called a business healing, in which I went to the enterprise to change the energy from failure to success. One of these appointments involved visiting a Guatemalan clothing and jewelry store. The prior tenants at this site owned a greeting card shop which had gone out of business. When I closed my eyes while visiting the new store, in my mind's eye, I could see the former owner holding his head in his hands in despair as he contemplated closing the doors forever. His grief permeated the walls, ceiling and floor of the location. I grounded and released the stuck emotions from the fabric of the building. I also noticed that the current owners had set the intention in the store as if it was their home, thinking that it was a comfortable place to be.

This belief was somewhat limiting, and did not allow for customers to come into the store, being that the shopkeeper, as well as most people, would not invite into their home everyone from off the street. Hence the entrance was psychically closed to customers. My students and I communicated this to the owner. We also filled the location with bright yellow energy that symbolized abundance to the proprietor and the employees. The next day, we received a phone call reporting that the company incurred record sales.

Once, during a healing on a flower shop, I intuitively read the feeling of dread from the previous florist, who wanted desperately to leave the floral market. He sold the shop to my client Terry who, for all her enthusiasm, hard work, and long hours, could not understand why this new venture was not profitable. After clearing the negative pictures, she was quickly able to turn the business around to a lucrative endeavor.

How the Poor Think

We have already learned that the rich can hold a picture in their mind's eye long enough for their energy to create it. The poor, on the other hand, send so many conflicting signals to the brain that it is impossible for the psyche to distinguish which image to manifest. Usually the idea starts out as a positive concept for a split second followed by a string of negative thoughts.

Also, the impoverished intellect often dispatches distorted and fragmented thoughts. These indistinguishable concepts confuse the spiritual part of the person, making it difficult to generate exactly what the creator desires. Therefore the originator ends up with an undesired outcome.

Stan (not his real name), who was essentially homeless and ended up sleeping on various friends' couches for several years, came to the abundance workshop and received a clairvoyant reading from me. During the session, I asked Stan to envision a car. As he attempted to form an image of a car in his mind, I did not see psychically any definite impression, strong picture, or a specific depiction of a car. In fact, there was nothing there, just contradictory thoughts and colors.

He said, "I kind of want a car, I think. Maybe I want a car but I don't know. Maybe a blue one. Maybe someone could give it to me, maybe not. I don't know if that will happen. I keep having to walk. I wish I didn't have to walk. I have to walk everywhere or borrow a bicycle. The other day, I had to cycle 17 miles to get to where I wanted to go."

Stan's representation of the car was not focused enough. He immediately followed his vision by creating too many conflicting negative images of what could happen for his energy and mind to generate the positive photographic representation. The image of the car was not distinct, nor did Stan stay focused on the positive image long enough before he started to fill his mind with the negativity of how he did not like to walk.

Stan also changed the image. This is typical of the poor who often make a blueprint or mock-up in their mind's eye, but keep changing it every few seconds. A person's powerful lifeforce energy cannot create the blueprint unless there is some consistency in the thought process.

The mind becomes confused as to which picture to formulate. An individual must think of a notion and hold it in the brain for a few seconds *without* thinking of the worst possible scenarios. The brain asks your consciousness, "Should the result be the negative fixation or the fleeting winning idea?"

You can start to change your thought process by visualizing the negative image disintegrating and by replacing it with the positive one. It is possible to change your thought process and start to create abundance. I told Stan to go home, cut out pictures of cars, paste them on a board, and look at it everyday. I also asked him to write down a paragraph about what it was like to drive his future car as if it had already happened, and to draw a picture of himself driving the car he wanted. After much work in changing his thought process, he eventually went on to own a car of his own.

The more concrete your thoughts are, the easier it is for them to manifest. Writing down a paragraph about how you'd like to live your life and then drawing pictures of it forces the mind to focus on the manifestation long enough to create it.

Let's do an exercise to put this into practice. Write down where you would like to see yourself in five years. Put in all the details, including objects you own, where you live, and the activities of a typical day in your life.

Now draw a picture. It doesn't matter if you don't have any artistic talent. Use stick figures if you must, but see yourself in the picture. This makes your energy create the desired outcome. If the picture is clear, your energy will start to generate it. Happy creating!

Chapter 16

When Will I Meet My Soulmate? Do Soulmates Really Exist?

OFTEN, AS I GIVE A clairvoyant reading, I am asked, "When am I going to meet my soulmate?" The timing of a future relationship can be read in a person's aura. The way I read this is by first looking at the seeker's aura as a color. Then I slide his or her energy along an imaginary timeline and I see if there is a change of color over a particular month or year, as I silently ask myself, "Is there a change?" If so, then good news—this person will meet a romantic match. If there is no change, and his or her energy goes along a timeline far into the future and off the timeline, then bad news—given his or her current activity schedule and energy, he or she is not on a path to meet a mate.

Don't worry—a future prediction is not always set in stone. You can change your future based on your thoughts and actions. This means that if meeting your mate is not on your direct path, you need to change your path and actions. Perhaps your soulmate lives on the other side of town, does not work at the same location as you, and does not shop at the same stores. You must increase your chances of meeting your soulmate by altering your current spiritual path by joining a singles club, church group, the Sierra Club singles, or post your personal ad online.

One example of this occurred when I gave a clairvoyant reading to a woman, Sarah, (not her real name). Sarah asked me, "When will I meet my tall, dark, handsome man?"

Clairvoyantly I moved her energy slowly along a timeline for her future life. After seven years, there still was no change in the vibration or color of her future, meaning that she would not meet her man within that time. I told her, "Given your current path, you will not meet him in the next seven years. So you must change your path."

The room was silent, then Sarah spoke, "You mean that I can't just continue to go to work, the ladies' gym and shop at the same grocery store to meet my match?"

"That's right," I replied. Sarah decided to adjust her schedule to include going to places that she did not normally frequent. She also joined some clubs and engaged in some social activities. As a result, she was able to speed up her path and meet her new beau, Mark.

Next comes the question of soulmates. I have read many people who asked me, "Do I have a soulmate?" I almost always see that people have more than one soulmate or spiritual lifetime partner to choose from who will help them complete their growth here on earth. I have seen up to twelve soulmates for one person. This doesn't mean that you must have a serious love-relationship with all twelve people! It merely means that you have many choices.

Some people can choose the soulmate who they want to spend their life with. A soulmate will help you complete your growth here on earth by providing an energetic agreement. Many people who help us grow will not be romantic partners, but instead will be your siblings, children, parents or teachers.

A soulmate can also be a spirit that was once united with you. You have split and become separate. Having a life together completes you and your mate. We are all of the same source, spirit, or a part of God. In a sense, we are all soulmates with each other. We are one, yet striving to find our own separate identity and unique vibration to become "pure of heart." Once we achieve this vibration, then we have truly reached enlightenment.

Will you be ready to meet your soulmate once you have changed your current schedule, path and actions? Not only do you need to change your path physically, but you also need to change spiritually, as well. The more "whole" you are spiritually, the easier it is to find your match.

The final question is, "How do you become whole as a spirit, and prepare yourself to be a great partner to your new mate?"

The answer: Clear your stuck thoughts and negative energies from your inner essence. Begin now to learn psychic tools to change energy and thought patterns in your electromagnetic field. Find a clairvoyant teacher to help you facilitate your growth and help you to start resonating at your highest vibration. This will make for fewer obstacles on your path towards love and will help you to attract your true companion.

Chapter 17

What Does Your Aura Reveal about You?

THE AURA, AN ENERGY FIELD extending about two feet around the body, has been referred to as "the window to one's soul." All living things, including animals and plants, have an aura made of energy. This energy radiates from the cells and the chakras, which are referred to as "energy centers." This energy produces color vibration.

Sometimes you can actually see a glowing color around a person's body. At a metaphysical church where I once worked, I often could see a golden light around the body of a teacher after she completed a meditation.

The coloring, shape, and size of the aura can tell many things about a person's personality, disposition, and thoughts. If there are multiple bright colors in the aura, then it shows that the individual has many interests. If there are only two colors in the aura, then often the person is focused on only two aspects in his life.

If you are constantly thinking about the future, your aura will extend out in front of you, and become thinner behind you. If you are often thinking about the past, for example—recalling your high school or reflecting on your college days—your aura will extend behind you. There is a tendency for certain cultures to hold their aura in a particular position. Here in the United States, our auras tend to be greatly extended in front of us, showing that our focus is on the future and what's going to happen next. In certain parts of Southern Europe, the aura of the older generation tends to extend behind them, as they remember a better time in the past.

The aura reflects your spiritual health, so if you are stressed, angry, or influenced by other's thoughts, this condition will be reflected in the aura as dark colors or bright white. If you are frequently tired, you might be extending your aura out to encompass the whole room. You then pick up energy from others, which lowers your stamina. If you become ill, your aura shrinks in size to assist in the healing process. Shrinking the aura helps to ensure that you don't pick up stray energies.

Energy isn't good or bad. It's either yours or not yours. It is as if each person has his or her own brand of fuel or energy. If you put your energy and thoughts into others, it might make them feel good for a while, but eventually they will not feel good because they are not being themselves. Energy works best if you have your own energy in your own aura. Having your own energy in your aura is reflected by vivid or pastel colors.

The positioning and size of the aura are not fixed and can change. An aura healing from a clairvoyant reader can release dark colors, holes and tears from the aura, allowing you, the spirit, to heal yourself. Once the spirit heals itself, the body starts to heal itself, hence the saying, *"Heal the spirit and the spirit heals the body."*

You can also learn to heal your own aura. One way of doing this is by learning to read the aura of someone else. When you learn to read someone else's aura, you start to process your own similar experiences. *You might become aware of shared experiences.* This is called a "Matching Picture." If you fell off a horse when you were 12 years old and the person you are reading also fell off a horse when she was young, then you have found a matching picture.

If you feel you have a matching picture with this person, then you can use the psychic tools of grounding or exploding a rose, as practiced in the clairvoyant program, to release the matching picture or thought. You free up your energy from this thought and you feel better at the end of the aura reading.

I once hurt my knee in a heated tennis match. Over the next two months, several of the people coming in to see me for readings had various knee problems. I got to look clairvoyantly at each person and see how each was handling their knee problem. I was able to release my "matching pictures" and become neutral to my own knee situation. Gaining this neutrality enabled me to heal my knee without surgery, just by processing the stuck energy in the limb.

"Can everyone learn to read an aura?" Yes, everyone can learn to read an aura. Many people already read auras, but they are not aware that they are doing so. They walk into the office and unknowingly notice that their co-worker has bright green in the second layer (the relationship layer). They just have a gut feeling that the co-worker is excited about someone in her life, and say, "You look good today."

The co-worker answers, "I got engaged over the weekend and I'm so happy."

This leads to the next question people ask me, "Is there a color scale for an aura?" meaning is there a set distinct meaning for each color. There is no color scale, but there are some universal color definitions.

The best way to give an accurate reading is to go within and come up with your own answer as to what a color means. See if a word or feeling comes to you as you concentrate on that color in their aura. See if a scene appears in your mind's eye of this person doing a particular activity as you ask yourself, "What does this color mean? What word or feeling do I get from it?" Don't just take someone else's color definition from a book you read, because then you don't end up giving an accurate reading with your own information and spiritual gifts.

Over the years, for my own readings, I have noticed that the color lime-green often symbolizes change or growth, especially if you have been experiencing a negative situation for your whole life, or at least a long time, and it has just been relieved or solved.

Red can mean enthusiasm, female energy, anger or the person's mother, but again it is best to go within and ask your inner voice silently to get the most accurate description of what the colors mean.

There are seven main layers of the aura that correspond with the main energy centers in the body.

Layer number one is next to the body. Layer number two is a few inches out from the body is further away, and so on, until you reach the seventh layer which is furthest away from the body.

Here is a guideline to the layers to help you get started in reading:

1. First layer usually relates to the body and environment, and often reflects your health.
2. Second layer relates to emotions or love-relationships.
3. Third layer relates to power and is often expressed in the seeker's work or career.
4. Fourth is the body-being layer, and often shows your relationship to your birth family.
5. Fifth layer would be the communication layer, conveying whether or not you have ease or frustration in your ability to communicate to others.
6. Sixth layer shows how you see the world, and your outlook.

7. Seventh, or outermost, layer is a sign you show the world. One might display colors communicating, *I'm happy. I'm sad. I'm capable. I'm scared. I'm intelligent.*

Here is an additional step to reading someone else's aura. It helps to close your eyes to help you tune into your sixth chakra and inner voice in the center of your head.

Ask yourself silently what color is the first layer of your friend sitting next to you? Listen internally for the answer. Let the first color that comes to you be the correct answer. Do not second guess or doubt your answer.

Now, ask yourself what does this color in her first layer tell you about her? (Again, the first layer relates to the body and the environment.) See if you get a sense or feeling or a word comes to you that describes this person's body or environment. Asking yourself silent questions aids in reading.

What word, feeling or image did you receive about this person? Perhaps you got the words "healthy" or "moving to a new house."

Congratulations! You have now taken your first step towards being a clairvoyant reader.

Chapter 18

Energy Cords: Why You Can't Get That Man/Woman out of Your Head

ARNOLD KEPT THINKING OF HIS ex-girlfriend, Mary, everyday for six months. It seemed that he had gotten over her, but then he kept thinking about her again and again. He didn't know it but he had an energy cord in his aura connecting him to Mary.

Energy cords are lines of energy that link one person to another, often connecting the energy centers or chakras. Cords get created when there is unfinished communication or for a purpose of giving or receiving energy. A cord can have three functions: (1) to receive energy, (2) to send energy, and (3) to send *and* receive energy. Some cords naturally disintegrate when the conversation is finished; those cords do not concern us. It's the cords that linger that can cause problems.

Beth was a manager in a software company. She had many employees needing her help on a project they were working on. The employees created cords going into her crown chakra to siphon information for the project, and into her third chakra to demand her attention. None of this would have been a big problem if the cords were removed a few seconds after they were created, but Beth went home and still felt as if she was at work. She even could "hear" chatter in her head when she closed her eyes. She constantly felt drained and did not know why. She was literally being drained by the energy cords in the chakras. At the institute, Beth learned psychic tools to gently remove the cords after the day's work by gently unhooking them from the chakras and tying them off. She also learned that she had thoughts in her aura and consciousness that allowed for people to cord into her. So she started to remove the thoughts. Thoughts are real and can act as a doorway for energy cords. Beth wanted to be available and helpful to her employees, just as, when she was the oldest child while growing up, she wanted to be available and helpful to the younger children. Through the use of some spiritual tools, she learned that she could still be supportive in the work environment without taking on other people's energy.

Cords have different meaning when they connect into different chakras. A cord going into your first chakra from another person usually means that they need something from you regarding survival—money, food, or security. Small children receive survival information from their parents or other caregiver. If this cord is severed, then the child is unsettled. The cord is naturally removed later when the child becomes self-sufficient and manufactures his or her own survival information.

Cords connecting the second chakra to second chakra in two people usually relates to attraction. A man or woman will send a line of energy into the other's second chakra if he or she is interested in that person. I once saw a married woman who experienced energy cords into her second chakra from single men, as she became turned on by flirtatious co-workers and grocery store workers. She did not want these cords in her second chakra because she wanted to remain faithful to her husband. She realized that she had thoughts and pictures stored in her aura from earlier in her life allowing these energy connections into her.

When she was 16, she had been quite homely and could not get a date to the prom, whereas her two older sisters were beautiful. She had a thought in her aura that *anyone's* attention was a good thing, no matter who it was. Later on she blossomed into an attractive woman and now she was inundated with energy cords. She removed the thought and was able to keep others' cords from going into her chakras.

What you cannot see can impact you, and it is fascinating to realize how much energy affects people. Often a physical problem can have an energetic cause. I once read a lady who had back pain. Clairvoyantly I saw an energy cord going into the back of her aura from her brother, who was going through a period in his life where he was experiencing fear and uncertainty because he had been laid off from his job. As a child, he had developed the energetic habit of attaching his energy to his older sister whenever he had been afraid. Now as an adult, he did the same thing. He unconsciously attached an energy cord into his older sister who now lived in another city, and he siphoned some of her energy to help him feel more confident. Meanwhile, his sister couldn't understand why she suddenly didn't feel as energized as usual. She started to feel drained and even needed extra sleep for no apparent reason.

To a clairvoyant reader, it was clear what was happening. A clairvoyant reader who knows how to use psychic tools could give this woman a healing and remove the energetic cord so she would feel energized again. Even better, this woman could take a class and learn how to heal herself so she could be self-sufficient and not need to go to the reader when she felt drained.

Conclusion

The following telltale signs let you know if you have cords in your aura:

1. You feel tired for no reason.
2. You continually think about someone even after they are not around.
3. You have a small rash in a circular pattern over your heart or on your neck.

Remember, cords can't permeate your aura unless you have a picture or doorway to allow it to happen.

Chapter 19

Spirit-to-Spirit Communication

NOTHING IS MORE POWERFUL THAN a spirit-to-spirit "Hello." Saying hello to people's souls is an acknowledgment to their essences, their energies, not to their bodies. This form of communication can be given by sensing the brightest color in their aura and saying hello to that as a vibration. This way of communicating can acknowledge a greeting in which you don't really want or need anything from them.

In the clairvoyant program, students learn to say hello to a person as a soul and not just to them as a body. One way students do this is by creating a gold rose, putting in the word hello, and sending it to someone in the room. Then they drain their energy off the rose so the salutation is completely neutral and without judgment. They then send it though time or space, imagining it going over to the center of the recipient's head. The gesture is one of appreciating of the spirit, saying, "Hello, I see you."

In fact, if you cannot say "hello" to someone because you are angry at them, you are stuck, and that person is free. This is not to imply that you must allow someone to invade your space or take advantage of you. On the contrary, if you can say "hello" to someone yet acknowledge that you do not agree with them, then you have freed yourself from being controlled by your anger. You have ended the cycle of non-communication with that person and liberated yourself with honesty.

When I was a student in training, I decided to try this out while driving my car. I came to an intersection and saw the silhouette of a man in the next lane, who was driving a pickup truck. His window was about two feet in front of mine at the intersection and he could not see me, and I could not see his face because of the positioning of our vehicles. I envisioned saying hello to this man's soul. The light then turned green and we both sped off to the next junction. I quickly let go of what I had done and started to think about other things. I turned and drove four blocks, and parked my car in the parking lot of my destination.

As I emerged from my vehicle, a man I did not recognize pulled up in front of me as I walked towards the sidewalk. He rolled down his window and inquired, "Excuse me. Did you say hello to me?"

I was startled. "Well yes, I did," I said as I suddenly recognized who this man was.

He smiled and asked, "What did you want when you said hello to me?" He seemed as bewildered as I was.

Lewis Bostwick, the man who started several psychic institutes in California, once attended a Renaissance Fair with his wife's family. Her brother-in-law told Lewis that he didn't believe in psychic abilities or in clairvoyance. Lewis usually wouldn't try to prove himself, but this time, he decided that he would. As the six of them made their way though the thousands of people at the fair, Lewis whispered into the ear of the brother-in-law, "Did you see that lady in the green dress who just walked passed us? I'll say 'hello' to her and she'll come back through the crowd to see us."

The brother-in-law rolled his eyes in sarcasm, murmuring, "I'll believe it when I see it."

Within a few seconds, the lady in the green dress tapped Lewis on the shoulder and asked, "Did you say hello to me?" The brother-in-law was shocked, and wondered if it was a trick, yet he had seen it with his own eyes.

Sometimes clairvoyant readers are asked, "How is it that you can read someone over the phone?" Because of the nature of spirit-to-spirit communication, looking at someone's body is not necessary. You can also speak to someone telepathically who is in another country. When a reader trained at the institute learns to read, he is asked to close his eyes in order to access the sixth chakra. However, closing the eyes also aids in tuning into the seeker as a spirit, and not to his or her body and how that person looks.

When I first was teaching clairvoyant classes, I would lecture in the evening but work at an office doing accounting in the daytime. My accounting boss, John, knew that I had a second job helping people to develop their intuition. He was also a Doubting Thomas, not believing that there was any validity to clairvoyance. One day while I was doing my work, John came over to my desk and started to invalidate the authenticity of spiritual abilities, even though he was a good Catholic. I, too, suddenly got the urge to play the game of "Prove It" with John. A few weeks ago, John had fired an employee named Steve so I told John that I was going to transcend time and space, contact Steve spirit-to-spirit, and ask him to call me at work while John was standing beside my desk. I tuned into Steve as a color; he was vibrating at a beautiful turquoise blue. I silently said, "Hello, Steve. Please call me at work."

John jeered and started walking away from my work area. When he got about ten feet away, the phone rang. I picked it up and it was Steve. In disbelief, John rushed back towards me and grabbed the phone from my ear.

"Steve?" he queried. After John realized it really was Steve, it became awkward, because he was speaking to an employee whom he had fired. He handed the phone back to me. Steve told me, "I was just sitting here at home and unexpectedly got the urge to call you."

Sending a spirit-to-spirit hello is not something only a few people can do; it can be done by anyone. But it takes some practice to truly give someone an acknowledgment without intention or energy attached to it.

Send someone a spirit-to-spirit 'hello' today and start to develop this for yourself.

Chapter 20

Can *You* Really Make a Difference in the World?

SOMETIMES WE DON'T DEVELOP OUR spiritual abilities because we don't really believe that intention, psychic energy or thought can make a difference in the world. While we were growing up, we were never taught that thinking or energy can change anything, so we don't make much effort to alter the world. However, numerous studies have proved contrary to this belief.

In Debra Williams' book *Scientific Research of Prayer: Can the Power of Prayer Be Proven?* she describes a study on germinating seeds done by Dr. Franklin Loehr, a Presbyterian minister and scientist, whose objective was to see, in a controlled experiment, what effect prayer had on living and seemingly non-living matter. One experiment used three pans of seeds. The first was the control pan. A second pan received positive prayer, and the third received negative prayer. Time after time, the results indicated that prayer helped speed germination and produced more vigorous plants. Negative prayers actually halted germination in a number of plants and suppressed growth in others.

In another experiment, two bottles of spring water were purchased. One container was used as a control, receiving no prayer; a group of people prayed over the second. The water was then used on pans of corn seeds layered in cotton, with one pan receiving the prayer water and the other receiving the control water. The pan receiving the prayer water sprouted a day earlier than seeds in the other pan. The prayer seeds also germinated faster and grew more quickly. The experiment was repeated, with the same result each time.

In his book, *Be Careful What You Pray For*, Dr. Dossey looks closely at experiments with microorganisms. He writes, "Skeptics who do not believe in the effects of distant intentions say that any observed result must be due to the expectation of the subject or to the power of belief and thought." Dossey argues that if bacteria respond to outside intentions by growing more slowly when prayed over, compared with control groups not receiving prayer, then one cannot dismiss this result by attributing it to negative suggestion. Bacteria presumably do not think positively or negatively.

Another major advantage of microorganisms in studies of distant mental intentions has to do with the control group. If the effects of intercessory prayer, for example, are being assessed in a group of humans who have a particular illness, it is difficult to establish a pure control group that does not receive prayer. The reason is that sick human beings generally pray for themselves; or outsiders pray for them, thus contaminating the control group, which by definition should not receive the treatment being evaluated.

In studies involving microbes, this notorious "Problem of Extraneous Prayer" is totally overcome because one can be reasonably certain that the bacteria, fungi, or yeast in a control group will not pray for themselves. Nor will their fellow microbes pray for them.

If the study involves negative intentions instead of positives, the advantages remain the same. The thoughts of microorganisms do not influence the outcome. Jean Barry, a physician-researcher in Bordeaux, France, chooses to work with a destructive fungus, *Rhizoctonia solani*. He asked 10 people to try to inhibit its growth merely through their intentions, from a distance of 1.5 meters, thus transcending the space continuum.

The experiment involved control Petri dishes with fungi that were not influenced, and other dishes that were influenced by thought. The laboratory conditions were carefully controlled regarding the genetic purity of the fungi and the composition of the culture medium, the relative humidity, and the conditions of temperature and lighting.

The control dishes and the influenced dishes were treated identically, except for the negative intentions directed toward the second set of cultures. A person who was blind to the details of the experiment handled various manipulations. The influencers simply took their stations 1.5 meters distant, and were free to act as they saw fit for their own concentration. For 15 minutes, each subject was assigned five experimental and five control dishes. Of the ten subjects, three to six subjects worked during a session, and there were nine sessions.

Measurement of the fungus colony on each Petri dish was obtained by outlining the boundary of the colony on a sheet of thin paper. Again, someone who did not know the aim of the experiment or the identity of the Petri dishes did this. The outlines were then cut out and weighed under conditions of constant temperature and humidity. When the growth in 195 experimental dishes was compared to their corresponding controls, it was significantly retarded in 151 dishes. The possibility that these results could be explained by chance was less than one in a thousand.

Another less scientific experiment was done in the Women's Intuition Class twenty years ago. A number of women were complaining about the limited birth control choices available, so a group of ladies got together and meditated and clairvoyantly looked at the scientists who were doing research on birth control. The women from the class removed the blocks for these scientists worldwide, and created the energy of many new contraception products to become available. In about a year's time, six new methods entered the marketplace. Coincidence? Perhaps, but there had been few new products in the four years before that, and suddenly six new products appeared.

Mass consciousness does have a large effect on planetary development. I believe that you should spend some time setting intention for the researchers working on new inventions, cures and solutions to reach the world. Your thoughts alone could be the bit of consciousness to help break through the barrier of the undiscovered answers to the world's problems.

Chapter 21

Beings, Entities, Ghosts, and Spirit Guides Demystified

"I AIN'T AFRAID OF NO GHOST" says the once popular song from the movie, *Ghost Busters*. So often I meet people who are afraid of these spirits or ghosts because they fear that these spirits have power over them. They don't even want to talk about the subject since they are so fearful of them. Those who originally had the ability to see beings as children start to turn off their ability to see entities, or they start to ignore them and pretend that they don't exist. They also think that if they acknowledge beings, entities or ghosts, then they might be closer to evil. Not all beings are evil. You are always senior to an entity in your own space. There are many types of beings, and *none* of them has power over you if you have the proper tools.

We humans are also beings. We are spirits who have chosen to occupy a body and incarnate here in this world. When we die, we become beings without bodies. Therefore, spirits without bodies are much like people; some are enlightened and some are not. Every being has personality and interests, whether in a body or not.

One of the myths about spirits is that they know everything, from the reason for our existence to today's winning Lotto numbers. In actuality, they are much like us, each having an expertise. They are able to transcend time and space and can reach other planes, yet most of them do not know what subjects are important to you or what is going to happen next.

Since beings, entities, spirits, and ghosts do not take physical bodies, people experience them differently, either by seeing them in their mind's eye, feeling their connection into the body, hearing their voices in the head, or occasionally actually seeing them with the naked eye.

Let's explore some of the various types of beings.

Healing Masters

These beings have an energetic agreement with us to give healings by changing energy in your chakras, or energy centers and your aura, the space two feet around you. The Healing Master can be trained to connect into the back of your hands and send neutral healing energy, which usually looks gold, through the hand chakras. This neutral healing energy cleans foreign energy out of you or the person you are healing (also called the healee or seeker). You, as the director of the healing, remain neutral. You do not need to use your own life force energy to heal, but instead let the Healing Master do the work. This creates an incredibly powerful healing, since you are acting as a vehicle for the healing to occur. Since the Healing Masters do not operate in the time and space plane as we humans do, they are able to transcend blocks, enabling us to boost our ability to heal ourselves.

The Healing Master knows about healing and we train our Healing Master about keeping their energy out of our bodies. Even some of the most enlightened spirits forget what it is like to have a body, and need to be reminded of simple rules to be most effective and operate safely. The Healing Master, as well as all other spirits, should be told to come in only when called, and leave when asked. No entity should have free reign over you to control your schedule or body. Of course, you can instruct them to come in and warn you of potential danger, and then leave after the warning.

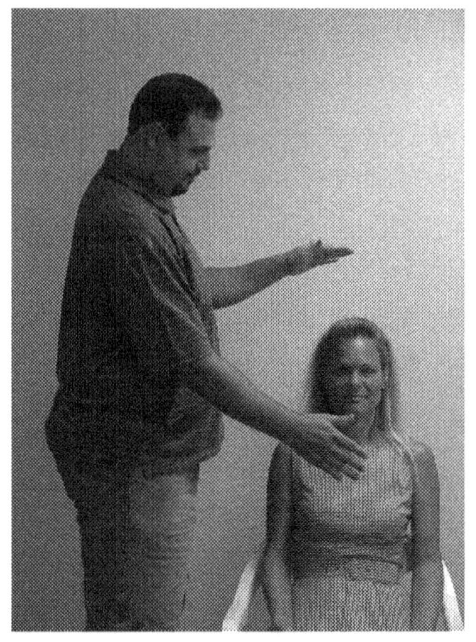
Working with Healing Masters

Healing Masters can be instructed to plug in only to the hand chakras and match your energy vibration, therefore making it easier for you to facilitate the healing. They should not come fully into your body, otherwise they tend to leave their energy in your body which can eventually cause disease or pain.

Spirit Guides

Almost everyone has spirit guides around them. Some of these beings are helpful. These beings can be experts at protecting you as a guardian angel, or they can help you find lost objects. Just like humans, they can be experts in particular topics. It is possible to outgrow your spirit guides and they are no longer serving or guiding you. You might ask, how could you outgrow a spirit guide?

Say you were an warrior in another lifetime who lived in South America several centuries ago, and you had a spirit guide back then who helped you fight. It would tell you where and when to strike, and would come into your body to help you fight. It was very helpful at that time. Then you incarnate in this body in a culture where killing someone is a felony. Your spirit guide is still with you and wants you to fight until death. It was really helpful that other lifetime and but it might not be helpful now. Agreements that are spiritual in nature tend to stay with you when you incarnate. You can imagine breaking the contract with a guide you have outgrown, much like tearing up a piece of paper that you both signed.

To better communicate with your guides, sit quietly and ground yourself to the center of the planet. Release any thoughts and clear your mind. Set up a chair across from you. Ask your guide to sit in the chair. With your eyes closed to help you access your sixth chakra, say hello to your guide and ask its name. The first name that comes to you is usually the correct name.

Angels

There's so much controversy about angels. Recently they are very popular, and are letting their presence be known. They are beings that have a special agreement with God, the Supreme Being, to help with certain situations, help a person grow, or help a person in a transitional time. Angels may intervene in suicides, help someone in distress navigate to safety, prevent a car accident, or help avoid a dangerous outcome.

Occasionally, angels will team up and form a group, called a council. These councils assist in guiding people on their paths, much like advisors.

Cosmic Cops

You can call them police beings or cosmic cop beings. About 1 in 100 people have a cosmic cop, usually people, who in their last life or the lifetime before, destroyed themselves or many other people. They were heroin or opium addicts, or they blew themselves up and everybody around them, or they did something so destructive that they've got one of these police beings who is not a guardian angel but a being that sticks with them and keeps them on the straight and narrow path. As soon as they start to go off their path, the cop just forces them back onto the path. These beings are not very polite or friendly; they have a job to do and they do it.

A lady named Barbara once came into the institute where I worked, accompanied by two of her coworkers. She and her two friends worked at a bomb factory. Barbara had been promoted to work directly on making bombs and suddenly developed narcolepsy, a disorder where the victim falls asleep unintentionally. The strange thing was that Barbara could stay awake most of the day, until she started actually working on a bomb. A clairvoyant student read her and discovered that she had destroyed many people with a bomb in a prior life and now she had a cosmic cop that would knock her out every time she started making a bomb, and made her fall asleep. The reader recommended that she change jobs.

Demons

Demons, devils and lower level entities do exist on the planet. When you learn psychic tools, you can have seniority over them and direct them away from yourself. These beings thrive on fear, pain, and punishment. The important thing to remember is that you, the owner of your body, *always* have seniority over your body. In other words, you are more powerful than them, so there is nothing to fear.

A good exercise to do when you encounter a lower level being is to imagine a line of gold energy and attach it to the crown chakra (at the top) of the demon. Give the other end of the cord to God, the Source. Ask the Supreme Being to take this entity away so you can be at peace. With this, the Supreme Being will respond and you can finish singing, "I Ain't Afraid of No Ghost!"

Chapter 22

Removing the Veil: Talking to the Other Side and Reconnecting with Your Loved Ones

WE LIVE IN A TIME where we are speeding up our spirituality. Everywhere on the planet, we are opening up to hearing about our past lives and our energy. You could say that we are in a Spiritual Renaissance or a period where we are unveiling what is hidden inside of us. We, as humans on earth, are becoming awake.

Another thing that is happening is that the veil between the spiritual and physical is being diminished, to the point that there is often no veil or separation at all between the other side and this side. They are becoming one and the same.

Popular mediums such as John Edward and James Van Praagh teach that your deceased friends and loved ones are trying to connect with you, sometimes once in a while, and sometimes all the time, and

I'd like to teach you some techniques so that you can do that without the help of a medium.

I have been practicing this spirit-to-spirit communication for many years, and some of my best teachers have been from the other side. They have instructed me how to hear them better while I was reading a client.

As a clairvoyant, the way I see it is that the beings who have passed over to the other side are at a different vibration than those beings who are currently occupying a body. It is a matter of either you changing your vibration to match them, or them changing their vibration to match you. Sometimes both beings meet on common ground, for example in your dreams, where it is easy for you to hear the deceased and for the deceased to communicate with you.

It is important to become clear so that you can hear the being that you want to connect with. If you are all cluttered up, then it is difficult to hear, and you start to put your own thoughts and impressions into the communication. Once, when I was speaking with a lady's deceased father, he told me that I had lots of energy blocking my communication with him. He told me to use the spiritual tools I had learned—grounding, running energy, exploding roses and being in the center of my head—to clean out my aura so that I could get the message for his daughter more clearly.

Remember, energy is never good or bad; it's just either yours or not yours. If it is yours, it works great in the body; if it is not yours, it can mess you up, make you unclear, or make you lose confidence in your ability.

To clear energy that is not yours before a reading, put your feet flat on the ground, take a deep breath, and then let it out. Close your eyes but don't drift off. Stay present and clear inside your body. Imagine a bright light at the base of your spine. This is your Survival Energy center (aka the first chakra). Now create a hollow tube connected to this spinning ball of light. Extend the tube down to the center of the planet. Anchor yourself and plug into the planet. We are now going to activate the gravitational pull. Feel the Earth's gravity pulling your body into the chair, and also pulling any energy out of you that is not yours. Imagine seeing stuck thoughts and energy draining out of you. Postulate that you're just effortlessly letting go of it. We're on a healing planet that absorbs with gravity and returns energy to a neutral state.

Once we release, we always want to replenish our energy field so that whatever we released doesn't get recreated. See a giant sun above your head. Postulate that this sun is a magnet bringing back your life force energy from all the places you have left it, from home, work, or from solving something. Bring it in and fill in the cells of your body.

Next we're going to get rid of energy blocking your clairaudience. Clairaudience is your ability to hear spirits. Most of the time, this ability is stored in your fifth chakra (your throat) and in the sixth chakra (your head).

Imagine a chair beside you, and call your deceased friend or relative by name. Imagine them coming into the room. (It's my experience that most of the time when I call someone, they come to visit.)

Teach your spirit visitor to talk to you from outside your head, meaning that you imagine a transparent plate of glass between you and your friend. That way, you are teaching them about space. You have your space and they have their space, as if you are in a bubble of your energy and your friend in spirit form is in his or her own bubble.

Sometimes, when you first start communicating with spirit, other spirits who you knew might be anxiously awaiting your communication. These others might have been waiting for you to be open to hearing them, and they jump in the way to try to get their message across. It's as if they are jamming the doorway to communicate with anyone else.

Don't resist this. I first talk to the anxious spirit to see what it has to say or show me. Then I go back to calling in who I wanted to speak with in the first place. I ask the being to change its vibration so that I can hear them. This might entail them lowering their vibration or matching my vibration. It's as if we both have a radio frequency that we tune into together.

Once I feel that they are tuned to my vibration, I ask for an identifying object or thought that would allow me to recognize that they are here. This thought should arrive in your mind in a matter of seconds. I often ask for a second identifying thought, for confirmation. You might experience them with: (1) "knowingness"—you just know that they are there, (2) seeing them with your eyes closed, (3) sensing their color, or (4) hearing them with clairaudience, or their thoughts enter into your mind. Whichever way works best for you, allow yourself to come into contact with them.

For example, when I speak to my mother, she identifies herself by showing me her hair, which was a very different hairstyle from anyone else's hair who I had ever seen. When I ask her for a second thought to identify her, she shows me a picture in my mind of the office she worked at in Texas.

I also do this when I am reading someone else. After I ground myself, clear my own thoughts, and replenish my own life force energy, I ask my client to tell me the name of the person they knew and their relationship. I often have them say their own name to me, too, so I can separate their energies out. Sometimes there is quite a bit of energy from the deceased person in my client's aura. I make a separate balloon next to my client for the spirit without a body to move over to, so they are not merged with my client.

The first time I practiced with a friend, I asked Linda, a friend, if I could connect with a dead relative of hers to see if she had any messages. She said, "Sure, would you contact my deceased Aunt

Luanne." I asked this lady to appear in the bubble I had created for her off to Linda's side. Once she appeared in the bubble, I noticed that her colors were bright, mixed with a pastel color. I asked her to show me a thought or photograph of something that my friend, Linda, could identify. Immediately, I got the thought of a blue china teacup.

When I told Linda about the teacup, she exclaimed, "It's on display in my china cabinet. That's the only thing my aunt left me!" Once I established that this spirit was her aunt, I asked her, "Is there anything you want to tell Linda?"

Aunt Luanne communicated not in words but in pictures and feelings, which are not always as easy to understand. She showed me that Linda's daughter would be okay in her new school, and that Linda would find a job soon and not to worry about finding it, otherwise the energy of worry would slow down the hiring process.

Linda told me later that she was sending her daughter to Catholic school and she was worried that her daughter would not like it, and that she had been seeking employment and was worried that she wouldn't find anything.

If the message is not so clear, do not invalidate yourself because often it's the messenger who isn't clear. Some are better communicators than others.

Once I was haunted with deceased poets who wanted me to put together a poetry CD of recordings of famous poems. After I recorded and distributed the CDs to poetry enthusiasts, the entities did not bother me anymore.

Extra pointers to communicating with the other side:

1. Tell them to visit you in your dreams or on the astral plane.
2. Give them a job to help you with, such as getting a raise, a date or a relationship.

Speaking to the deceased improves with practice. You can practice by yourself or with your friends. Speak to as many of your friends' deceased relatives as possible and say hello to them from me!

Chapter 23

Jesus Appeared in Aura Photography

AURA PHOTOGRAPHY IS A WAY of taking pictures of the non-material world with a special camera. It provides a way of viewing the unseen patterns of energy and force fields that surrounds all living organisms. Some claim that the technique can serve as a medical diagnostic instrument, too. The beauty of aura photography is that it makes psychic phenomena real.

Aura photography is not to be confused with Kirlian photography in which a living thing is placed in contact with the film. Leaves of plants and fingertips are the common contact points in Kirlian photography.

In aura photography, the subject holds a sensor in each hand, or places the hands on metal sensor plates, and the camera superimposes a representation of the subject's aura on a Polaroid photograph.

When I worked for a psychic institute in Northern California, we put on psychic fairs almost every weekend at various locations around the San Francisco Bay Area. At a psychic fair in Golden Gate Park, many people wandered in, bought tickets and got a reading. My friend Pat was in charge of the aura photography. A girl I'll call Barbara was fascinated with the aura photography but was a devout Catholic and had been taught that anything not Catholic was considered a sin. As she put her hands on the electrical sensors, she closed her eyes and started quietly chanting repeatedly, "Dear Jesus, be with me here. I praise and love you. Bless me as I go through this process."

As Pat waved the drying Polaroid in the air and the picture got clearer, she glanced at the photo, and then stared at it with wide-eyed astonishment. It seemed that Jesus had appeared in Barbara's aura, over her left shoulder. Pat was speechless! Finally, she managed to squeak out, "Look!" as she showed the photo to Barbara.

Barbara looked at the photo and jumped up and down with excitement. "I'm loved. I'm loved. Jesus came. He loves me." She grabbed the photo and disappeared into the crowd to find the girlfriend she came to the fair with.

Pat could barely talk because she had a new level of belief in her abilities as a result of the photo. This was as much of a surprise to her as it was to Barbara.

The game of trying to convince the world that psychic phenomena are real is difficult since non-believers unknowingly direct their energy to create the results they want to see, thus not getting a positive outcome. But for Barbara, for Pat, and for the group of clairvoyant readers, the photograph was real.

Chapter 24

Why Did You Lose That Object?

CAN'T FIND YOUR KEYS, your cell phone, your wedding ring? There's often a reason you can't find it. Sometimes energy collects on objects, just like energy collects in a location.

Once I was getting ready to go to a meeting at work and couldn't find my car keys. It was really important that I get to the meeting because a conflict was brewing between me and a lady I'll call Carol, and I needed to make it to this meeting to clarify a decision that would affect room assignments. With only four minutes to go until the meeting, I sat down, breathed deeply, and went within. Immediately I saw that Carol's energy had come into my aura to prevent me from attending the meeting. Her energy had attached to my keys, so I grounded them by connecting a hollow tube of energy to help release, and saw the dark blue drain off them. I then visualized the keys and wrote my name on them. Next, I ran an elastic energy cord from my third chakra to the lost keys. I suddenly "saw" them in my mind's eye on my coffee table under some papers. I lifted the papers and voilá. I drove to the meeting and prevailed in the conflict.

Psychometry is the art of reading the energy on an object. It is an ability that uses a combination of the sixth and seventh chakras, plus the chakras in the palms of the hands. Antique dealers are often great psychometry readers. They can "read" the energy off of an antique desk or jewelry. Also, if you were raised in a household where your siblings used your toys and things, leaving their energy on them, often you have a higher tendency for psychometry and you may have inadvertently developed it more than most people.

A friend once inherited some costume jewelry from her grandmother. As she and her sister split up the jewelry, they were excited at the prospect of wearing these unique pieces. A year later, the sisters were conversing and the subject of the inherited jewelry came up. Both admitted that they were unable to wear a single piece of it because of the energy stuck in the metal (an excellent carrier). They decided to clean off the energy by grounding the objects and imagining the energy releasing into the planet to be absorbed and neutralized. Then they wrote their names energetically on the jewelry and "owned" it for themselves. Lastly, they brought in a gold vibration and imagined the neutral, bright golden energy engulfing the metal and stones. Instantly, they both felt okay about wearing the jewelry.

If you inherited an object or piece of jewelry and you cannot seem to use it or don't feel right about having it in your house, probably there is some old energy clinging to it. Also, if you lost something and cannot find it, then that object has collected energy from someone. Sit down, close your eyes, center yourself by grounding, and release all the thoughts in your mind. Imagine the object out in front of you. Imagine that you are placing a tube of energy connected to the object and connected to the center of the planet. Allow the energy that has collected on this object to dissipate down to the earth to be neutralized. Finally, fill the object with a golden vibration of energy and write your name on it with an imaginary pen. It is now yours, and should be easier to use or find.

Chapter 25

What Are the Akashic Records?

YOUR AKASHIC RECORD IS A record of everything you have ever done, all of your past lives, everything about them, and the original blueprint of your body. Even information about the future can be found in the records. To most clairvoyants, the Akashic records appear differently. Some psychics see the Akashic records as a library with books about everyone and everything, from the life of Benjamin Franklin, to the purpose of onions, and to everything that has ever happened on the planet.

In this library, every soul has its own book, and you can therefore access information on anybody else. You can also access information on any topic. Also, certain beings or spirits act as "librarians," called Akashic record keepers. Their job is to organize the records and make sure they remain intact, and everyone has one assigned Akashic record keeper. In the clairvoyant program, students are trained to look at each other's records rather than accessing their own records. This makes sure students are safe from causing any damage to their own records.

In the records are also columns of energy, or cycles that you've completed. For example, if you had many lifetimes spent in poverty, you may have a column of information devoted solely to what you learned by being poor.

The Akashic record keeper will often give you a symbol for communication—it might be a red ball or a blue dinosaur. The record keeper will communicate in your mind's eye; for example, you might be instructed, "Put this symbol in your third chakra. This is missing information from a past life where you had the same injury. This symbol will help heal both lifetimes."

There is no mystery about the Akashic records. Anyone can learn to access them. I often caution students about accessing your own records because there is a great temptation to want to rewrite them. It is best to access someone else's records and allow someone else to access yours.

At times, I use the records when I'm giving a healing. For example, if you're reading someone who has a really bad back injury, you can go to the Akashic records for that person and obtain the original blueprint of how their spine was before the accident. You then bring that information into their body, which can use that information to heal itself.

Chapter 26

Using Your Telepathy

TELEPATHY IS THE ABILITY to send and receive thoughts from other people. The telepathic channels are located just above your eyebrows near the original hairline and the area just below the eyes at the top of the face. These are connected to the bone just behind the ears that protrudes from the head.

Once, as I was sitting in a writer's group, a fellow writer, David, decided to test my psychic abilities by telepathically asking me to pass the cookies to him. Again and again, David sent the message, as I was concentrating on the current writer who was reading his works. I received the message but thought it would be rude to interrupt the man reading his work to see if David wanted some cookies. Finally I couldn't stand it anymore and just handed the bowl of cookies to David, who was amazed.

Another time, I had a co-worker named Phil who worked next door at the publishing company. We would have conversations without using nouns. Our conversations would go like this:

Phil: "Are you going to pick up the ..."

Vessa: "Yes, then I'm going to ..."

Phil: "That will be great."

Vessa: "I'll bring ..."

Phil: "Good."

Each of us understood the other and satisfactorily turned and walked away. Most people have at least one or two people around them with whom they have a telepathic link—it might be your co-worker, your spouse, or your best friend.

Telepathy can be a frequency, and tuning to the frequency can open up a communication line. Because there is no time or space to spirits, it can be over a long distance or across the room. We are all spirits and it is just as easy to communicate across the continent as within a classroom.

Telepaths get jammed up with the countless messages you get in today's culture. "Buy this car!" "Don't say that!" and "Don't eat my pizza!" are just a few of the messages you get daily from various people. People with sinus troubles are often incredible telepaths, able to pick up or send messages to others with extreme clarity, but the gift comes with a price.

If you clean out the telepathic channels, you can receive more current messages. Here is an exercise to help you clear out your telepathic channels so you can have increased telepathy:

1. Image two miniature roses attached to your index finger. (We will use these symbols of roses to absorb stuck thoughts from others that are jamming your telepathic channels.)
2. Touch your skin right above the eyebrows moving from the center of your forehead over the eyebrows to behind your ears. As you do, see in your mind's eye the tiny roses clearing the channels of any energy blocking your ability to send or receive a thought.

3. Envision "hanging up the phone" on people who have been sending you messages, and imagine telling them to call you on a physical phone. Watch out! Your telephone may ring within the next hour.
4. When you have repeated the previous step for a few moments, then move the rose outside your aura and visualize the rose disintegrating and releasing the purified energy to the universe.
5. See golden energy replenishing your temples with light.
6. Send an image to someone you love and see if he or she responds.

Enjoy using your telepathy for sending and receiving images and thoughts.

Chapter 27

The Myths of the Chakras

IN THE FAR EAST, spiritual leaders looked clairvoyantly at others and saw seven spinning lights in a person. They discovered the circles to be energy centers of the body. There are seven main in-body chakras, then minor chakras in the hands and feet. The outside and inside parts of these energy centers spin two ways—clockwise and counterclockwise. The Eastern religious leaders clairvoyantly saw these energy centers and named them with the Sanskrit word *chakra* translated as "wheel."

1. The first chakra is located at the base of your spine and is the size of a fifty cent piece. This chakra handles the survival of the physical body.
2. The second chakra is located two inches below the navel. This chakra is your emotional energy center and also houses sexual information. It houses your clairsentience, which is your ability to feel what others are feeling. Have you ever had a "gut feeling" about something? Then you are probably using your second chakra.

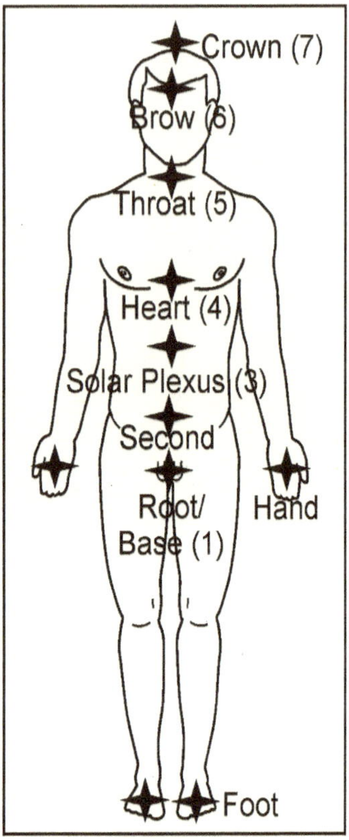

3. The third chakra is located in the center of the body about five inches above the second chakra and is your power center. Most people use their third chakra in the work environment to assert themselves. It is also the chakra of dreaming and astral travel.
4. The fourth chakra or heart chakra is located over your heart and is often called the affinity chakra. This is the chakra of love. With this energy center, you can experience from mild to extreme forms of love.
5. The fifth chakra is located in the throat and is your communication center. This chakra is often used for telepathy—hearing and sending thoughts.
6. The sixth chakra is in your forehead and is the chakra used for clairvoyance and intuition.
7. The seventh chakra is located on the top of your head. Unlike most of the chakras which are cylinder shaped, the seventh chakra sits like a crown on your head, hence it is often called the crown chakra. The seventh chakra contains information about precognition—the ability to tell the future, and trance mediumship—the ability to channel energy.

Chakras open and close the way a camera lens operates. Contrary to popular metaphysical belief, it is not beneficial to make your chakras open up as wide as possible. When doing readings, it's good to close down the lower chakras to help you get more of your energy up into your sixth chakra in the center of your head. Close down the lower chakras to about 10%. This closes off survival information temporarily.

A healthy chakra should open and close as the information from that chakra is needed. For example, if you step in front of a truck, the first chakra should open to 100% to help you access survival information and tell you to get out of the way. Then when you get safely back on the curb, it should start to close down, somewhere below 50%.

If you are constantly worried about money or where your next meal is coming from, then your root chakra will surely open to 70% as a normal percentage, but if you have enough to eat, are emotionally happy, and know where your next paycheck is coming from, then your root chakra will reside at about 25% open — a healthy percentage for someone who has his or her survival needs met.

Besides directing your chakras to remain open, another way they get jammed opened is if you receive a physical blow to the head, if you drop acid or take drugs, if you have had psychological trauma, or if you have trance mediumship ability. All of these cause the chakras to get stuck open.

When people take acid or other hallucinogenic drugs, for example, they begin to tune into other planes of consciousness that don't match our plane of consciousness. They cannot readily distinguish what is happening on this plane and what is happening on another plane. They might become afraid of something that cannot hurt them here because it's on another plane.

Another myth about chakras is that they are permanently a certain color. Chakras can change colors, and be of different colors in different people. To arrive at the correct color of a chakra for a person, intuitively ask your inner voice, "Is this the optimum color of this chakra for this person?"

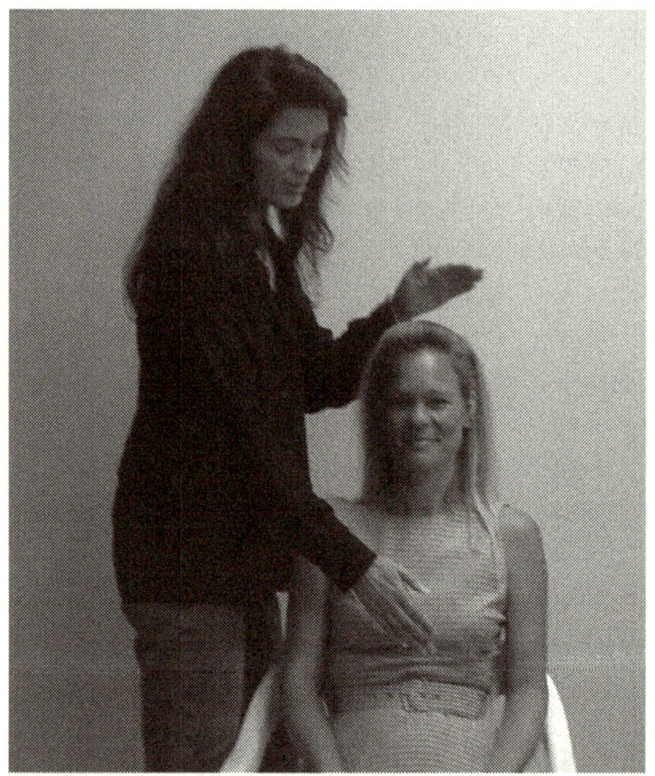

Working with Chakras

Chakras can get cluttered up with thoughts and energies from other people. Here are the types of foreign energy usually found in chakras:

1. If the first chakra is not working correctly, you may have absorbed energy from someone else. One of the most common foreign energies found in the first chakra is from people who depend on you for their survival. People who owe you money or want to borrow money from you, animals or pets that you take care of, people who depend on you because you are housing them, or people who depend on you emotionally tend to collect in the first chakra. The only foreign energy that should be in the first chakra is for people who have small children—in which case, parents should have an energy cord into their child's first chakra to share information on surviving.

2. If the second chakra is not working correctly, you may have allowed in energy from people who are attracted to you, or past lovers from a long time ago.
3. If you have pain in the third chakra area, it may be caused by foreign energy in your third chakra, such as energy from people who are competitive towards you.
4. The fourth chakra is the one that collects the most energy if someone who once liked you is currently enraged with you. If you are experiencing pain in the fourth chakra because someone is angry with you, then imagine untying the energy cord (see Chapter 18 on Energy Cords) and sealing off the place where the cord entered.
5. Types of foreign energy in the fifth chakra are energies from people who want you to say something, or occasional spirit guides who will try to speak through you. (This is a common occurrence with many people.)
6. Sometimes people who want to influence your viewpoint of the world will put their energy in your sixth chakra. For example, if you are an editor, they want you to miss a phrase. Sometimes people will put energy in your head out of curiosity to see what you are seeing, or perhaps someone wants you to view the world from their perspective and not your own.
7. Foreign energy in the seventh chakra might include energy from people who want to know what you are thinking, know your information, or want to control where you are going.

What can you do about foreign energy invading your chakras? You can imagine the foreign energy as a color and see it gliding down into the center of the planet to be neutralized. Direct your chakras to start spinning once again, with your own bright colors in each.

Chapter 28

Which Dichotomies Are You Living?

MY CLIENT ANNE WAS UPSET because she did not want her daughter, Marcie, to go through the pain of a broken heart. Marcie was dating her first boyfriend and he suddenly seemed uninterested in her.

Although it is understandable to not want your loved one to go through pain of any kind, if you allow them to have experience, it brings forth the knowledge of dichotomies, both the positive and negative. From this awareness, you can create a better future for yourself.

Sometimes we need to experience both sides of a dichotomy to appreciate life and to know the positive dichotomy. For example, it is difficult to know total happiness if you haven't experienced sadness, or to appreciate love when you have never experienced a lack of love or emptiness from loneliness.

A great example of dichotomies is the story of Buddha. Buddha was born into a rich family and resided inside the palace walls, secluded from seeing anything that was contrary to the riches and luxury of a prince's life. He lived contently experiencing a lifetime of gluttony, indulgence, and extravagance. One day, the gate to the palace was left open and he ventured out to discover the very poor and those who suffered. He soon renounced his family, leaving the palace in disgust, intending to face life's other extreme. He proceeded to deny the body, forcing himself to survive on a single grain of rice per day. He punished his body, imposing fierce conditions of heat and cold, until one day, while meditating under a Boddhi Tree, he realized that penalizing his body was not the correct path to becoming an enlightened soul. He discovered that if he were able to stay in the middle of the road, he could have both ends of the dichotomy without being stuck on one end or the other, and in doing so, he could reach the illumination of his psyche.

A similar message appears in the Bible where Jesus puts forth the question, "What if a man gained the whole world and lose his own soul?" If you have gained the whole world and obtained all material wealth, but have lost yourself in the process, then really you have gained nothing. If you are stuck on one side of a dichotomy, be it riches or poverty, you are not free.

All people experience dichotomies in life, for example, being happy versus sad, being rich versus poor, being healthy versus sick, to name a few. Other dichotomies could be love and hate, fat and thin, beautiful and ugly, good and bad, sane and insane, smart and stupid, happy and miserable. To experience a dichotomy means to get closer to what you want to have.

An exercise in the clairvoyant program helps you reach a resolution about a question you may have been contemplating. Perhaps you are trying to decide about two sides of a dichotomy. For example: "Should I keep my current car and fix it, or should I buy a new one?"
"Should I leave this job or count my blessings and stay here?"
"Should I keep this cat or give it away?"

"Should I stay in this relationship or leave?"

First, sit comfortably in a chair with your hands in your lap, palms up. Then, put the two sides of the dichotomy in your hands. We are going to examine it three ways.

1. One hand at a time, pretend that it's already happened. If you are trying to decide whether to keep the car and fix it or buy a new one, pretend that you have already decided to keep it. See yourself with the same car as if it has already happened.

2. Now, ask yourself how you feel in this scenario. Do you feel happy with the decision?

3. Lastly, see how this decision affects others and how they are reacting to your resolution. Who does this affect? What's the reaction of your friends and your family now that you have decided to keep the same car?

Next, pretend that you have decided to get a new car. Envision yourself as already having purchased it. How do you feel about this new car and the payments? What's the reaction of your friends and your family now that you have this new vehicle?

Now, go back to where you were before and become neutral again. Implementing this exercise enables you, the spirit, to go completely into the dichotomy, then climb completely out of it again, allowing you to see the middle road. You become spirit, rather than being the problem you are trying to solve. It should now be easy to come to a conclusion about your next step in this matter.

Chapter 29

Matching Pictures

WHEN I WAS WORKING AT a job several years ago, I observed a secretary (I'll call her Amy) who worked for three attorneys. Amy had a series of thoughts or pictures in her aura of "fear of not doing a perfect job." She had absorbed this thought from her childhood experience with her father, who had told her that she did not work hard enough no matter how much work she did around the house.

Overall, she performed well in her career and seldom made mistakes in her work while handling the requests of two of the three attorneys. However, the third attorney had the picture in his aura that "secretaries make mistakes." It was an image he created based on his previous experience at another law firm, in which several of the administrative help made errors in their work for him. When he came to the new law firm, he brought his energetic baggage with him in his aura and started manifesting his reality.

Together this attorney and Amy had a match of their past experiences. She started to unconsciously assist this attorney in manifesting his expectations by performing sub-par work for him and by making silly mistakes for no reason. Even though Amy rarely made mistakes with the other two, she just could not seem to get it right for the third lawyer. This is an example of manifesting a reality based on the thoughts in the aura. Matching pictures are experiences that you've had, which are similar to, or interlock with, the experience of another person.

In a clairvoyant reading, readers spend time de-energizing matching pictures. Perhaps you are a schoolteacher, computer programmer, or bank teller, and you decide to enroll in the clairvoyant training program. One day, while practicing giving a psychic reading during the healing clinic at the institute, you give a clairvoyant reading to a man who took a fall from a horse as a child. Earlier in your life, when you were about eight years old, you also had an experience of falling off a horse. Perhaps even now you are afraid of riding a horse. If this experience were a traumatic incident, then there would be an energetic "charge" on the thought, and energetically, it would have gotten stuck in your aura. If you use psychic tools to de-energize the event of falling off the horse, then the result is that you no longer are afraid of horses. Imagine putting the image of you falling off a horse into a rose. Now explode it.

De-energizing matching pictures is one of the main reasons for taking the Clairvoyant Training Program. Therefore, it is best to read a person who has similar experiences in life as you have had in your life. When you first learn to read using the spiritual tools taught in the clairvoyant program, these images start to get released from the aura.

If someone is bothering you in your life, you may be working on a matching picture from an earlier experience. Spend some time today and visualize releasing the matching picture through grounding it out and exploding it in a rose. Free your energy from being stuck in the past.

You can learn something from every person. If you can't say, "Hello," you are stuck, not that you have to let that person in your space.

Chapter 30

Dreams

DID YOU KNOW THAT WHEN you dream, you actually leave your body and enter the astral plane? You always leave a percentage of your energy (about 30%) in the physical body to maintain it, while the other 70% of you leaves through the chakras to work things out on the astral plane. When you are on the astral plane, you occupy your astral body, which looks very similar to your physical body. This spiritual body is connected to your physical body by the "silver cord" at the third chakra, which is a strong line of energy acting as an anchor to keep you connected. During your sleep, if you hear a sound or some foreign energy enters your room or body, the body sends a signal via this silver cord to you, the spirit, to come back quickly, and usually you then jump awake immediately.

Leaving the body at night is a necessary process to keep you alive and healthy. You, the spirit, need a break from being in the lower vibration of the body. Also, the body needs a break from you, the spirit, so it can rejuvenate itself. When you dream, you also dump all the thoughts from the day out of your head. It goes through part of the consciousness called the "analyzer." Everything you thought about during the day or week dispenses here.

"Are all dreams real?" many have asked. The astral plane is a free-for-all place to work out issues affecting you. It is a safe place to experience a situation without repercussions. For example, you can meet and be friends with famous people, you can date your boss, and you can even experience what it is like to die in a dream without harm to your body.

There are two types of dreams. In the first type, you go through the analyzer and dream about silly things that happened to you during the day. If you were doing your laundry, then you may dream about missing socks. You literally remember mundane activities while you process out these thoughts from the analyzer.

The second type of dream is where you really make it onto the astral plane and you see old friends, relatives, and get a chance to experience. These are genuine dreams — not associated with mundane daily activities. You are using the astral plane to grow, change and experience as a soul.

What if you have a dream about the future? Are all future predictions real? The answer is "No." You can control your own future. A dream is only an illustration of something that may happen, but does not have to happen. The future is formed by individual and group consciousness. (See Chapter 3, *Who Controls Your Future?*)

The astral plane has twelve distinct levels. For example, on the seventh and eighth levels, spiritual leaders teach to enlighten those of us in bodies. The arena of learning healing and spiritual information takes place at the Cathedral of the Souls. To get there, merely tell yourself as you get ready to go to sleep that you would like to go to this special place. It might take a few tries before you get there, but if you ask to go there, eventually you will end up in this arena. You will be in a lecture or participate in a healing experience.

You can also receive an answer to a question you have by asking it before you go to bed. As you drift off to sleep, simply pose a question to which you want the answer. Envision that you will get the answer in your dreams. This is called conscious dreaming. When you wake up, you will know the answer. Remember, it may take a few times before you get a response.

Chapter 31

Tea Leaves, Runes, I-Ching and Tarot

OBJECTS THAT SPIRITUALISTS USE TO give readings are really an extension of reading the aura. In most cases, the reader uses the object (tea leaves, runes, Tarot, I-Ching) to bring out his or her own intuition.

The former owner of the Ryder-Waite Tarot deck reproduction rights, Linda DeMenno says, "One of the best ways of reading Tarot cards is to throw away the manual on how to read them and use your own intuition to guide you. This way, you give a more accurate reading than memorizing the book."

One of the most fantastic things about using tangible guides is that you can read yourself and you don't need a psychic around to confirm it. If you have a big decision to make, you can meditate and clear your mind, then consult the I-Ching, Tarot cards or rune stones.

I once went to a Halloween party dressed up like the stereotypical gypsy with dangling earrings, a bandana, several bracelets, over-done make-up, a crystal ball and Tarot cards. People I had never met jokingly came up to me and said, "Read me!" I played along and had them choose a card or I gazed into my crystal ball, then I proceeded to give them a reading that changed their life over the punch bowl.

One of the great things about using cards is that people focus on the cards and do not direct their attention into your head. Often psychics have trouble reading when the seeker focuses too intently on the center of the psychic's head, thereby making it difficult to be in the center of their own head to access their own answers. The seeker's energy enters into the psychic's aura and blocks the flow of information and energy. This does not happen as much when you use divination tools.

The object is not as important as the reader. This reminds me of a story when I was helping to oversee a huge psychic fair in Santa Cruz, California. My job at this fair was to direct the crystal ball booth, take tickets from seekers and assign them to a reader. The crystal balls were brought to the fair by my friend Lou, a fellow psychic. The fair ran until 7:00 pm, but Lou had an earlier appointment in San Francisco and needed to leave at 5:00 pm. Instead of waiting for the current eight readings to finish, he entered the booth, scooped up each crystal ball and slipped it in a velvet carrying bag. Then in an instant, he flung the bag over his shoulder, said, "Good day," and rushed towards the exit.

I had known Lou for many years and I had learned that when he wants to exercise his will, it's best not to intervene. The infuriated psychics, along with their upset clients, stopped the readings and looked at me as if to say, "You're in charge! Do something!" With that expectation, I quickly whipped out a pair of scissors and clipped the strings tethering balloons to the sign over the booth, and placed one balloon on each table between the psychic readers and their clients.

For a second, both the clairvoyants and the seekers stared at the balloons, and then the silence was broken as the readings continued with just as much enthusiasm and validity as before. Behind me were four more people lining up for their balloon readings.

Next time you are in a Chinese restaurant having tea, stare into your neighbor's tea cup and use the pattern of tea leaves to access your intuition and read your first impression.

Chapter 32

Core Pictures

SUPPOSE YOU'RE FURIOUS AT YOUR son's soccer coach because he pulled your son out of the game without, in your opinion, good cause. You react by refusing to let your son play soccer with that coach again even though your son is open to going back to ball practice. Without realizing it, the event that happened to your son stimulated an exact match of an incident that happened to you earlier in life, when you were unfairly told you could not play sports as a child. If your reaction to a situation is ever out of proportion to it, you could have stimulated one of your own "Core Pictures." A core picture is a thought or series of thoughts buried deep down in your subconscious mind.

Some people who have the same thing happen again and again are working back through this and are almost to the core picture. Somewhere in the aura, either the space two feet around you or actually in your body, lie thousands of core pictures. These thoughts are buried under other lesser charged thoughts. Your energy goes through these core pictures and creates a similar situation at some later point. To get the core picture out, you need a way to process it, a psychic tool to de-energize the original thought. You don't even need to know what the original issue was, but you can absorb it into a rose and explode it, and replace the core picture with a neutral golden energy. (Another way to process core pictures is to go through years of therapy, in which case you will need to find the exact thought at the root of your behavior in order to change.)

The next time you are furious or are experiencing extreme emotion over an incident that does not seem that critical, ask yourself, "What happened to me earlier in my life that reminds me of what is going on right now?" See if you can find the core picture for yourself. Once you have the awareness of the core picture, you are halfway there, because you can now release it and move on.

If you are not aware of the picture, removing the thought is more difficult. That's where the magic of psychic tools comes to play. If you are aware that you are hitting a core picture, but are not sure what it is, then you can imagine releasing whatever thought or thoughts are being stimulated in your consciousness, down a grounding tube to the center of the planet. Remember that to avoid the same energy getting recreated in that place, fill it with golden energy when you have finished.

Some core pictures get created at a very young age, even while you are in the womb or shortly afterwards. I remember giving a clairvoyant reading to a lady whom I'll call Barbara, who asked, "Why did I become so angry when my boyfriend tried to feed me cake yesterday?"

I saw the energy of a parent feeding Barbara with a spoon when she was a child. When Barbara got finicky and refused to eat the food, her parent would tease her and start to feed her, and pull the spoon away quickly, to entice Barbara to be more aggressive in eating. This caused her much aggravation as a young baby.

Years later, the core picture resurfaced when Barbara was interacting playfully with her boyfriend. Luckily she knew what to do and she de-energized the image using the psychic tools of grounding, erasing, or exploding a rose. She released the past aggravation, and could playfully let her boyfriend feed her.

As a clairvoyant reader, I inadvertently dig up many of my own core pictures as core pictures come up in my clients. I believe this is the best thing about giving a clairvoyant reading because a reader who has clairvoyant tools also processes his or her own issues while reading a client. After the session, the clairvoyant feels terrific because he or she has released many of his or her own core issues.

My favorite example of de-energizing one of my own core pictures happened during my clairvoyant training when I was attending part two of the Psychic Tools and Healing Class. The instructor asked us, "Blow up a balloon and imagine putting into it energy you are ready to release as the balloon expands." I had always had a problem blowing up balloons because every time I tried, the side of my head would ache, I would see stars, and then tears would stream down my face. I remember countless children's parties in which we youngsters were asked to inflate a balloon and I never could, even though I always tried hard. and ended up crying in the corner. Imagine the number of core pictures I had acquired over the years of my youth.

My psychic instructor pointed out that the pictures or thoughts were stored in my fifth chakra around my throat. He assured me that using spiritual techniques, I could rid myself of the images and blow up a balloon. I believed him and, after three weeks of class, I imagined exploding the stuck images in my throat and in my aura. Then, nervously, I tried to expand a balloon. It worked! I was able to blow up the balloon in its entirety. To this day, when someone asks me to help inflate balloons, I still remember the pain I had, but it's only a memory that no longer controls my actions.

May you have the same experience and euphoria in releasing your core pictures.

Chapter 33

Aliens, UFOs, & Visitations

I WAS ASKED TO SPEAK about unidentified flying objects and ETs at a psychic faire several years ago because I'd had many experiences with ETs and UFOs over the years. I asked my teaching assistant to accompany me to the workshop, but she seemed nervous. She told me that although she did not believe in UFOs or ETs, she was extremely afraid of them. I knew instantly that she'd had an encounter with ETs before, otherwise there would not be such an extreme reaction.

We have shared the earth with many types of ETs, although most of them have the ability to travel inter-dimensionally and can operate on this plane or another plane. It is difficult to fully understand that which we do not participate in. I have noticed that the ETs come to earth at particular times—mostly when the earth or mankind needs help or the planet is in danger. There are many types of ETs—some helpful, some harmful. Most of my experience with them has been beneficial.

In addition to the visitors' craft, the United States government has also manufactured a huge UFO that is housed in Arizona. It looks like a giant boomerang and it has three clusters of lights. One of my friends who used to be an aerospace engineer said that he would get some information from friends at Area 51. He described the U.S. government UFO as a manned V-shaped craft, with each wing moveable and 1½ miles in length. It uses stealth technology and magnetic propulsion (based on a Tesla design) so as not to show up on radar and it can hover, yet travel from the U.S. to Australia in seconds. He has footage of the Belgian Air Force chasing this craft. At night, all you see are the six lights on the leading edge of the wings, as in the famous Phoenix Lights sighting. Other U.S. craft are filled in, to give a delta-shape.

Many people believe that we were genetically engineered about 50,000 years by ETs who had colonized this planet. The ETs combined their DNA with that of a primitive Earth being called *Homo erectus*, to produce workers for the mines and fields. Evolutionists claim that we evolved from apes, and Creationists claim that God just put us here. The third, or Intelligent Design, group claims that ETs guided and sped up evolution so that modern man appeared far sooner than would normally have happened.

I once taught a class/workshop about ETs and discussed the appearance of aliens and their modes of transportation. More than one person had had a dream in which she was pregnant and then she wasn't. About 2 years later, she had a dream that she was on a spacecraft and her baby was there but was sick. After she spent time with the baby, it got better. She then had to leave ... and woke up. Hearing about the dream freaked out the people in the institute to the point that I was asked not to have that workshop again. If you talk about ETs and UFOs, chances are that you have had some kind of encounter.

I taught a spiritual class on UFOs at the psychic institute I worked at several years ago. One of the first exercises I had the class perform was to draw a personal experience with UFOs or aliens, no matter how crazy it seemed. I distributed crayons and paper, and asked that the students quietly draw or write, but not share their works with the others until everyone had finished their drawings. After a few minutes, I had everyone hold up their picture at the same time. To our surprise, nine students had produced a drawing of the *same* spaceship, and the other eight had drawn themselves undergoing the same operation performed by aliens.

My teaching assistant, Leslie, told me before the workshop that she was intrigued yet terrified of the concept of aliens. While she was talking to me, I could see clairvoyantly yellow energy around her head. I told her that if she wanted to remove the energy, she would once again be able to see UFOs and aliens. During the workshop, she concentrated on sending a rose through her brain, consciousness, and aura to collect up the yellow energy. Then she exploded the rose to disperse the hypnotic energy. (If you have taken the clairvoyant program, use your tool of erasure to clear this energy.)

If you are afraid when this topic comes up, it probably means that you have had an encounter and the memory was covered over using hypnosis. (Stuck hypnosis energy keeps you from seeing ETs and UFOs, so put it into a rose and erase it.)

Scan both sides of the brain, looking right under the 6th chakra for a wavy line of energy, usually yellow. If you find any, just erase it by attaching some neutral purple energy, putting it in a rose and exploding it. Then bring in a golden sun energy to reclaim those places.

Sometimes there will be an implant in your head or elsewhere in your body. Ground and run energy, and ask the Supreme Being (not the ETs), "Is this a beneficial thing or a harmful thing?" If it's not beneficial, you can take it out. It might just be a tracking device. In fact, most contactees have some kind of tracking device. You take it out or leave it. Use your intuition to decide what to do.

Chapter 34

Breaking the Cycle of Trance Mediumship: Why Are You Moody?

DO YOU KNOW SOMEONE WHO is extremely moody? Does this person say something and cannot remember that she said it a few minutes later? Then you might be interacting with a trance medium. Trance medium behavior was common in ancient society as well as in modern times. In the Bible, Jesus speaks of many episodes of spirits occupying a body.

Not all trance mediumship is bad. Edgar Cayce, also referred to as The Sleeping Prophet, was a trance medium. He had an ability to go to sleep and allow another being to come into his body. The other being, who I'll call Dr. Gehri, would diagnose people and give cures for terminal illnesses. He cured thousands of people and produced many books to heal future generations.

Catholics have the ritual of exorcism to take out evil demons. Psychic tools of grounding, connecting into God, and laughing with amusement can help in clearing out foreign entities. Even eating a healthy meal or taking a hot bath can help in releasing a spirit from your body. Also, getting out of pain will help you get re-anchored into your body. If the body is out of pain, then you will be more likely to occupy the body.

There can be some positive things about trance mediumship. Trance mediums are usually not bored, because they can create drama. There are even some trance medium cases in which people invite in another spirit. A few of these are ventriloquists, impersonators, and actors and actresses

Energy is not good or bad, it is just yours or not yours, meaning that you want to have your own energy in your body. If you allow another spirit into your body, and that spirit leaves its energy in your body, then you will eventually have health problems. This is why some trance medium healers die at a very young age.

I watched a grandmother interact with her grandson. She recognized that his behavior was suddenly erratic and his eyes changed. "That's not the Steve I know," she told him.

Once, an inner-city school teacher attended spiritual classes I gave. She could identify that many of the troubled youths in her class had other entities occupying their bodies with them. She could not verbally tell them about this because she would be fired, so she came up with a creative way to handle the problem. She stood at the door and looked at the eyes of the students. Those who had entities in their body, she stopped and said, "You can't come into the classroom yet. You have to figure out why," and went onto the next student. She ended up with three youths standing outside in the hallway, and they learned to keep the entities out while they were in her classroom.

Not only spirits can come into your body, but friends, family members, and even pets can climb into your body. I knew a lady who purchased a horse. After a few weeks of riding, she started to think like the horse. When she saw lush green grass, she imagined how good it would taste. The animal had entered into her head and was living there with her. She learned psychic tools to move it out of her head, so she could have her own thoughts back.

If you don't feel like yourself, then you probably have someone else's energy in your body. Don't worry. Removing beings is an easy process. Keeping them out for good is more difficult.

Another sign of trance mediumship is epilepsy—a disease caused by entities. A foreign spirit enters into a person's body. The beings that come in and cause a seizure are usually very primitive in nature and do not know how to correctly operate the body, hence the inability to speak or function during an epilectic episode.

One of the common signs that you are a trance medium is if you start sounding just like your mother or father. Guess what, you are probably channeling some of his or her energy. Pregnancy is a trance medium experience. The spirit that is ready to incarnate starts to hang around the expectant mother. Sometimes the being will come into someone else's aura, around the eyes, especially the left eye. If you have an uncontrollable twitch in your left eye, then you have a baby being around you. Baby beings do not care whether you are old or young, or male or female. Have you ever heard the saying, "a twinkle in your father's eye?"

To rid yourself of the flickering in the eye, imagine a sheet of glass off to your side. Ask the being to move to the other side of the glass. Tell it that you do not want to have it in your aura and body at this moment, and ask it to move out. Envision replenishing your aura with golden light to fill in the space that the being once occupied.

Chapter 35

Spiritual House Cleaning

A HAMBURGER STAND OPENED ON the corner of Clairemont Avenue and Kerry Street. It seemed like a great location, with a lot of drive-by traffic. There was plenty of parking and no other eating establishments around except for a nearby pizza place. The proprietor thought this business would be a cash cow.

The owner knew the fastfood taco joint that had stood on this site before the hamburger restaurant had gone out of business but he reasoned that perhaps it was that no one in the area liked Mexican food. Unfortunately, however, business was not good and he had to close the doors after eleven months.

Over time, other entrepreneurs opened businesses on the site—a Euro-fusion restaurant, a chicken place, and a sandwich shop—and failed. Have you ever known a commercial location where whatever business starts up fails, even though the site gives the impression of being excellent? This often occurs because the energy is set at the time of the first failure in this particular place, and unless the energy is changed, any new business will struggle.

Some new business owners inadvertently change the energy of the store as they open it, but most just put up a pretty sign and change the decor, while the energy of the previous failures remains in the location. Negative energy can be in the walls, floors, ceiling, furniture, carpet, and even in the foundation. I have even seen ghosts of Native American Indians who inhabited the land many years ago affecting a modern day business.

At Intuitive Insights, we train students in how to give business and house healings. The same negative energy can reside in a house. Some houses are actually haunted by spirits that have not progressed to the other side. They still have an issue that they are trying to resolve, and cannot move on without a healing. These stuck beings can affect the people who live in the house

There are many things you can do with a house healing. I know some former students who started a psychic real estate cleaning business, in which they read the energy on homes that have been up for sale for over two years. They clean the stuck energy and set the property at a new vibration. With a house healing, the property usually sells within a couple of months.

When there are spirits in the location, psychic house healers look to see if they are helpful or harmful. Often they will leave an angel or spirit guide from God, whose soul purpose is to keep the negative energies out. These beings are called "Marias."

One healer saw, stuck in the walls, the energy of a construction worker who'd gotten injured on the job. Sometimes the neighbors' energy gets into the property. In one healing, the energy of fairies from our ancient fairy tales was in the overgrown yard. Sometimes there is no need to move out all the foreign energies if the energy is not affecting the tenants in a negative way.

How to Heal Your Own House

Imagine going outside of your house. Ask yourself, "Who controls the energy in this neighborhood?" Who sets the tone? Is it a military neighborhood? Is there a big church or ashram setting the atmosphere? Is the ambiance set by a neighbor? That's good information to know in order to reset the vibration.

Imagine the foundations of your house. Just ground the foundation and let out all the energy of the people who have lived in that space. Let the gravity pull out all the people and their energy, and just see them out. Go ahead and clean out whatever is in your house and let that energy go into the earth. Replace that energy with golden energy by filling it with a golden sun. Gold is a neutral high vibration.

Look at each room in particular. What kinds of pictures and energies are in the walls, ceilings, floors of each room?

Start to fill the house up with gold energy. If you have any pets or other people in your house, say hello to them. Tune the energy to vibrate in affinity with you, your animals, and the other people who live in the place.

Scan for any spirit guides. Are they helping you or hindering you? For simplicity, you can just connect them right into the Supreme Being as if you are plugging them into a light socket, and have the Supreme Being take out the ones who aren't helping.

Bring a golden sun into your house. Imagine that you are setting the tone now. Tune it to your crown chakra, whatever color you have in your crown. Fill up each room. Ask God for a Maria guardian being, announcing, "I'm going to put a Maria in here to keep the energy from coming back."

Chapter 36

Energy Whacks

AN ENERGY WHACK IS THE same as a physical punch in the face, only with energy that can go into your aura, causing rips, tears and holes. Or the energy can permeate your body, disturbing your chakras and body functions. If it gets into your body, it can create pain, disease, emotional distress or loss of creativity. The phrase "if looks could kill" applies here. Whacks from males look like tears or cannon balls; female whacks look like BB holes or bullet holes.

Giving whacks is also known as "throwing energy." Technically, you allow a whack to happen by resisting to it or having a thought in your aura which acts as a doorway for energy to get into your space. A whack is a glob of energy thrown at one of your pictures or thoughts. When all of your pictures or thoughts are neutral, no one can control you or whack you. For example, Christ walked unharmed through an angry mob ready to kill him.

When Patricia was a child, a neighborhood boy teased her and told her she was ugly. Later after she grew up and was quite attractive, one day one of her co-workers told her, "You don't look that good today. That outfit makes you look frumpy." Normally Patricia would have not allowed his comments to bother her because she knew she did not look frumpy and this was just his opinion. However, his statement stimulated some past thoughts that she had never released from her aura dating back to her experience with the neighborhood boy. She became angry and hurt at the fellow worker's remark. If she had not had that thought in her aura that acted as a doorway, the whack would not have been able to get into the aura.

What to do when you get whacked? First ask yourself what past experience got re-stimulated. Clean out the energy thrown by the other person by absorbing his or her color into a rose and exploding it. Seal up any holes or tears in the aura. Bring in golden energy to replenish the energy you lost through the whack. If you are tempted to throw energy or whack back, refrain. Tune into your higher consciousness, and work on yourself. After all, the person who whacked you served you by showing you where you still have issues from your past to work on. Practice running energy daily and you will heal up any whacks, tears or holes in your aura.

You can also prevent yourself from getting whacked by not being in a resistant space. This is the first step in developing the body-of-glass tool of nonresistance taught at the Intuitive Training Center. Start to develop your nonresistance by being amused, jovial, and in a humorous mood. When you are in the vibration of amusement, very few energies can penetrate your aura and hurt you. You start to be invincible.

Chapter 37

Telepathy and Advancement with Animals

HAVE YOU EVER WONDERED ABOUT the evolutionary path of animals' souls? I believe that animals are on their own evolutionary path, separate from the human path. Dogs reincarnate as dogs, cats come back as cats, and so forth, unless they change their vibration while they are in a body.

Animals are here to teach and heal us, while at the same time, matching our vibration long enough to elevate them off the animal cycle. Even zoo animals are working on their own spiritual advancement.

Animals are spirits, as are humans. This is why we can communicate on a spiritual level, and send and receive messages. Animals can also be healers, sometimes absorbing the emotional pain we experience during the day. They, too, help us with our growth and transition from one issue to the next.

Animals also have astral bodies. After a pet dies, it often comes back for a few days. When you contact a pet, imagine greeting your pet as a spirit, by seeing its color. If your cat or dog died, call its spirit to the side of your aura, and ask him to bring his vibration down to match your energy so you can hear, see or experience him better. Imagine seeing the color of his aura. If you see blue, then envision saying hello to the blue energy.

Now the cat or dog can "speak" to you through images, so you can understand a being who does not always use words. See if you feel the joy or healing energy from him. Allow him to go back into the light to heal himself and invite him back to help you in the future.

In pet readings on animals who were put to sleep by their owners, I have never found that the dog or cat held a grudge about being put to rest. Most deceased pets were just happy to have their former owner speak to them again out of the guilt they were harboring.

I discovered at the age of five that animals think in pictures as opposed to words. My cat Mitten would think a thought of me putting a bowl of cat food down in front of him. At first I thought I was just anticipating that he was hungry but soon he started sending me other pictures that were not as obvious.

I remember him telepathing a picture to me while I was in my room playing. He was in another part of the house, and I distinctly received the thought of me opening the front door for him to go out. I went down the hall towards the front door of the house, and there he was sitting and staring at the door knob. This type of telepathy continued for a few years until Mitten disappeared one night, and my family and I never found him.

Later when I turned 10, my family traveled to California to visit Universal Studios, where many animals performed tricks such as raccoons opening soda cans. In a gift shop, I saw a book titled *How to*

Train Your Cat to be a Television Star. Hmm, I thought, *I wonder if I could send a picture from my mind to my cat?* I was excited to return home to New Mexico to experiment on the cat.

When I arrived home, I bent a metal wire into a circle about one foot in diameter. I called my cat and got a packet of special cat treats as motivation. Picturing the cat jumping through the hoop and receiving his reward, I shouted, "Jump!" The cat went through the hoop, and was rewarded with a treat.

After teaching the cat many such tricks, the most amazing feat happened when I told the cat to shake hands as you would tell a dog. I pictured myself shaking hands with the cat, and said, "Shake." The cat complied and placed his furry paw into my hand. When I closed my hand around the cat's paw, I received an image in my head that my hand was "dirty" and to "let go of my paw." The communication was not in words, but in pictures. I understood the cat immediately, so let go of his paw. I looked at my hands but couldn't see any dirt. However, I was certain that the message came from the cat.

I then got the idea to communicate back to the cat in pictures, that I would again say "Shake" but not close my hand around his paw. I said, "Shake," and he immediately put his paw on my palm as I raised and lowered it without closing my fingers around the top of his paw. We had a trusting two-way communication, and he earned his reward.

In conclusion, the first step in communicating with your animals is to believe that you can do it. Then send an image or picture through time and space to start the conversation.

— Taken from Vessa's book *Changing the Pecking Order*

Chapter 38

Why Are You Trashing Yourself?

TRASHING YOURSELF CAN BE ONE of the most destructive spiritual habits that you can do to yourself because it makes you go backwards spiritually. There are several reasons why people get into a pattern of trashing themselves.

It could be that you learned this from someone you admired, such as your mother, father, friend or a teacher. Perhaps you didn't want to appear egocentric or self-centered, so you trashed yourself to appear humble. Perhaps you think that putting yourself down makes you a better person and elevates you spiritually. Possibly someone in your family trashed you or you observed the adults around you trashing themselves. The pattern gets started at a young age, and you might have gotten validated for trashing yourself when someone told you that you are a good person if you transgress against yourself.

I have even met people who learned in traditional church services that trashing yourself will prevent you from being a bad person, as in the biblical admonition, "Judge not lest you be judged." The same should be applied to yourself. Maybe you can catch yourself and stop judging others, but when it comes to judging yourself, you don't give yourself the same courtesy. In fact, punishing yourself will make you a *less* spiritual person, since you will not be happy.

When I was a pastor of a non-denominational Christian church, I practiced speaking and listening to God and to Jesus. I learned from their responses to me that God wants us to be happy. You are sinning against God if you do not allow yourself to experience joy, happiness, and love every so often.

Learning self-love takes practice. Many people do not like their body and constantly send negative thoughts to it. Your body has its own form of intelligence and hears your communication. It responds to disapproving input by self-destruction or creating health problems, as it is calling out for help. Therefore, it is in your best interest to send positive thoughts to your body. If you think your body is too fat, then embrace it and love it anyway, as you help it transition to a thinner you.

Suspend judgment of what is good or bad about yourself, both as a spirit and as a body. Do not trash yourself for your experiences because there is always a reason that you created life's learning lessons. Your experience and mistakes are often how you grow. Every experience you have had has served you in some way, even the difficult and upsetting ones. Ask yourself what you have learned from these negative occurrences and see how you have grown.

Start to allow yourself to see all the good you have created in the world, no matter how small. For example, perhaps when you wake up in the morning, you bring a great vibration for the world. Perhaps you set a healing environment for your plants. Perhaps you bring forth a tone of justice and peace in your routine daily activities. Find out what you have learned from those negatives and see how they have served you. Focus on the positive aspects of yourself and radiate love.

Chapter 39

Suicide

ROBIN WILLIAM'S CHARACTER IN THE movie, *What Dreams May Come,* chased after a woman on the other side who had committed suicide. She could not hear, see, or even know he was there trying to communicate with her. She was just focused on the pain she had caused others while she was alive.

This particular scene, unlike the rest of the movie, was a surprisingly accurate depiction of what actually happens to those who commit suicide. They cannot see anything but the event of their suicide and the pain it caused others. They must relive it again and again until they realize the full extent and consequences of what they did.

Most of the time, when people want to attempt suicide, they have personally known someone who has committed suicide, and have absorbed thoughts and energy from them as a healer. These thoughts collect in the crown chakra and resurface again later in life, leading them to consider suicide when circumstances look grim.

Having a body is a tremendous accomplishment in the world of spirit, since there are trillions of spirits and only a few billion bodies. Only the most capable of spirits can obtain a body. Owning a body puts you on the accelerated growth path. If you are a spirit without a body and you get stuck on a thought, you may be stuck on that same thought for centuries or an eternity, whereas spirits who occupy a body must give into some of the needs of the body, such as drinking water, eating, and using the bathroom. When you do these simple acts, you stop focusing on the stuck or depressing image for a few moments, and you start to realize that this troubling thought is not you, the spirit, but merely just a thought.

Ironically many spirits without bodies convey the message that it is better to be in spirit form without a body than to incarnate into a body. I have even seen lower level beginner beings tell trance mediums that they should kill their body and join them on the other side in order to reach enlightenment. These evil beings occasionally plague those who are susceptible to hearing voices. In order to not fall victim to these beings, it is important to learn to distinguish between your own inner voice or thoughts, and the voices of those who are sending you silent, telepathic messages. It is also necessary to regain your seniority, knowing that you are more capable than these mischievous beings. Knowing that you are senior to these negative messengers enables you to send them away by commanding them to leave … and many times, they will depart.

A person with proper spiritual tools can assist the person who committed suicide in getting beyond the issues they are stuck on so they can progress. The first thing to do is to find and explode the thoughts the deceased person is looking at by envisioning a rose and have that rose absorb all of the beliefs in the aura. Clean these thoughts out by imagining that the rose is collecting up all of the thoughts of suicide, which take the form of orange or rust colored squares. Once full, move the rose out one foot in front of you and explode it.

To heal those who have killed themselves, first ground them. Then put a cord from them to the Source/God, and ask that they be energized. Clean out the chakras and aura by using a rose. Have the rose absorb dark spots in their aura; these are self-punishment thoughts. Clean them out and explode the rose. Say hello to them and listen for an answer back.

Chapter 40

Advantages of Developing Your Psychic Abilities

DEVELOPING MY PSYCHIC ABILITIES WAS something I had never considered while growing up in the deserts of New Mexico and Texas. However, I didn't realize it at the time, but I was naturally intuitive. At the time, the thought of being psychic, clairvoyant or intuitive meant to me making objects fly through the air at will, being able to know someone's future, and reading other people's minds.

Later I learned that being psychic or clairvoyant could mean many things. For example, "intuitive skills" include knowing what motivates or stops a person from achieving a goal, being able to read a person remotely from a distance, finding out where a person is heading in his or her future, and being able to heal and influence people without touching them. There was so much more to learn about using my natural clairvoyance that I hadn't considered.

As a teenager, I moved to California to attend college. A few blocks away from the U.C. Berkeley campus was a psychic institute which was also a non-profit metaphysical church. There, I received a clairvoyant reading that was so surprisingly accurate that I decided to temporarily delay finishing school in order to attend a year-long, intensive clairvoyant program.

The program changed my life. I became much more sure of myself and realized that I could do most anything. A couple of the telekinetic episodes still stand out in my mind, even though they happened several years ago.

During the clairvoyant program, I landed a job in San Francisco and commuted by bus from the East Bay over the famous Oakland Bay Bridge. One day after work, the owner of the company held an impromptu party at a local restaurant. I had to leave the party early to catch the last bus home at 7:00 pm. I arrived at the San Francisco bus terminal at 6:55 pm, and stood in line with three other patrons. By 7:10 pm, the four of us realized that the bus probably wasn't coming. I had no other way of getting home since BART (the subway) didn't go anywhere near my house. A man at the next bus stop told us that the bus had come and left early at 6:50 pm, and that we had better find another way to get home.

Undaunted, I created an energy mock-up taught to me at the clairvoyant center. This consisted of making a three-dimensional representation of what you want to have happen—in this case for the bus to come back and take me home. I released all of the energy surrounding this thought form which said that the bus' return was impossible. I energized the mock-up with neutral gold energy and asked God or the Supreme Being to bless it. Then I let go of the mock-up. The thought drifted out of my aura to go be manifested. After a few more minutes, the other passengers said that perhaps the man at the next stop was correct and that the bus really had gone. We started to lose hope.

Suddenly, the bus appeared. The door opened and the three of us got on a vehicle full of angry people. The driver admitted, "I got to Treasure Island (the half-way point of the Bay Bridge) and I got the urge to turn around and come get you. I realized that I'd left the station early. Despite all these angry passengers who wanted to get home, I turned the bus around on the island and came back for you, which I've never done before!"

We said, "Thank you!" The puzzled driver reiterated as he shook his head, "I've never turned around like that before for passengers." I smiled, knowing that my energetic mock-up had reached this bus driver to create a true miracle in my universe.

Although that seemed very spectacular, another incident really made me a believer in psychic abilities. A few months later, I changed jobs and started working in the East Bay at the federal courthouse. Again, I commuted to work by bus. One sunny afternoon, I was walking to the bus stop and I realized that I didn't have exact change for the fare. In fact, the only money I had in my wallet was a $20 bill. I started looking for a shop where I could get some coins or smaller bills but they all had signs in the window proclaiming: ***No change given without purchase.***

I thought, I don't want any food or soda. All I really want is a glass of water. (This was many years before the age of selling bottles of water. Back then, the only liquids for sale were sodas and milk.) I went into a store and decided to get a can of diet soda. I paid for it and received my change for the bus. As I held the soda in my hand, I thought, "I wish this were water."

I popped the can so I could drink it quickly before the bus arrived. Oddly, it tasted like water not soda. I poured some liquid out into my hand, and it was as clear as water. At that moment, I realized that it really *was* actual water. One could say that this was either an unbelievable coincidence or that my energy helped change the soda can into water.

Soon there were so many strange miracles that I could no longer dismiss them as coincidences. I continued my training and today help others realize the incredible abilities that we all possess in developing our God-given abilities. It is only a question of learning the tools, asking the right questions, and practicing what you have learned.

Chapter 41

You May Be Psychic, Not Crazy!

WE'VE BEEN TAUGHT THAT ALL the thoughts in our heads belong to us, but the truth is that much of what occupies our minds can be thoughts and emotions from others. You might be standing in line at the grocery store and start to pick up the thoughts or feelings of the person standing behind you. Now, suppose that person behind you is angry; you came into the supermarket in a good mood, but as you stand in line, you begin to feel angry. Your anger mounts and as you leave, you're furious with everything and everyone.

If you are a healer, often you will unconsciously pick up other people's energy if you don't have any psychic protection. What determines how much energy you pick up depends on whether and how you use the tools to keep you from absorbing thoughts and energy.

How do you distinguish which thoughts are yours and which are not? One way is by reading other people, and getting validated by them. Beginners may start out reading an aura and thinking that they're guessing but, in reality, if you use psychic tools to clear your energy field, and you access your sixth chakra, then you *will* see some of the thoughts of the person who sits in front of you.

If you have deranged, weird, disturbing thoughts, then those thoughts are usually coming from outside your energy field. Many lower astral plane beings generate deranged thoughts. Higher level spirits, such as your guides, also create thoughts and images for us but usually of a positive nature. Even our deceased relatives send us messages. I know a man who wanted to start to take spiritual classes at an intuitive training center up north. When he thought of this idea, he suddenly became paranoid that someone was in his kitchen cabinets. He opened the cabinets and, of course, no one was there. He became confused because he had never been a paranoid person and he felt silly having such strange thoughts. He later learned that he had a spirit guide who he had outgrown sitting in his aura and did not want him to go to the intuitive training center for fear of being discovered. So it caused all sorts of odd thoughts and weird distractions to stop him from going to the institute and finding the guide. He finally overrode the bizarre thoughts, made it to the clinic, and had a reading from a gifted clairvoyant who was able to remove the disturbed guide.

We pick up thought patterns from our family more easily than from strangers because our family is familiar to us. I know a lady who lived in California whose family on the East Coast started each day by reading the Bible and praying for her salvation. They prayed that she would return to the religion of her youth and leave the psychic mumbo-jumbo that she had started as an adult. This energy blocked some of her natural inborn intuitive ability. Every time she would start to give a clairvoyant reading in the training program, she would only see white and nothing else. This white energy was the color of the prayer energy encircling her head. She had to move out this energy using grounding and other psychic tools so she could start to do readings.

Mental institutions are filled with people with excessive spiritual sensitivity to hearing seeing and accessing alternate planes. Also, many adults and children who are on drugs really have a problem that can be helped with a spiritual reading and healing—problems ranging from depression, suicidal tendencies, fibromyalgia, Epstein-Barr disease, paranoia, agoraphobia, hearing voices, having unhealthy thoughts, and many other ailments.

I remember during my training as a clairvoyant, a fellow student had a child who was severely autistic. He came to the trance medium clinic four times over six months and reduced his problem enough so he could start to mingle with other children and adults. He grew up to function normally in the world. His mother also took classes to learn to more effectively deal with her son's issues.

In a beginning psychic abilities class, students first learn to clear their own minds by releasing stored thoughts using psychic techniques of grounding, running energy, and exploding the absorbed thoughts in roses. Once students have used these techniques, they can start to distinguish between thoughts that are foreign versus those that are self-generated, and they begin to heal the spirit which in turn, heals the body.

Chapter 42

Competition: The Spiritual Four-Letter Word

THERE IS PROBABLY NO ENERGY more destructive to a spiritual person than the energy of *competition*, defined as: "negative energy directed at you from someone who does not want you to do, experience, appear a certain way, or succeed at what you are already doing." (To me, competition is *the* four-letter word of spiritual profanity.)

This is not to say that there is any problem at all with physical competition. Physical bodies can enjoy competition and the effort that goes along with competing. Triumphing in golf, tennis, ping-pong or baseball can be pleasurable and euphoric. The challenge of competing motivates athletes to excel and strive for physical prowess that they would not attain in the absence of competition.

How does one exist in such a competitive world? The answer to competition is not to avoid it altogether or cloister yourself or your children from experiencing competition. A way to assist you in dealing with competition is to arm yourself with the tool of awareness that others are behaving the way they are because of competition.

Once while working at the phone company, I remember a beautiful, slender, enthusiastic, young lady I'll call Amy having extreme difficulty with a new supervisor. This overweight and homely new manager singled Amy out and was excessively cruel to her. Although Amy's work was equal to or better than that of her co-workers, the boss did not seem to criticize or antagonize any of them. After several weeks, Amy started to take her boss's insults personally, thinking her work was sub-par, which negatively impacted her self-esteem.

Seeing what was going on, I took Amy aside one day and told her, "You know, it's obvious to me that our new boss is jealous of your enthusiasm and appearance. It's that simple. I suggest that you don't take her comments personally. Perhaps put in for a transfer to another department, since she's let us know that she's planning to stay here for the rest of her career."

Fortified with this information, Amy was able to stay working for the jealous supervisor until she obtained work in another department a few months later.

The world is filled with competitive people, and resisting them only draws them to you. If you experience the feeling of competition towards you, try to find a way to deflate the competition. For example, my friend Carol went to an incredible bra sale at an upscale department store. The brassieres were only $5, which was a great price, and a hoard of women was digging frantically through the bins of bras, determined to find their size. The lady next to Carol was so desperate that she literally grabbed a bra out of Carol's hands. Appalled, Carol was about to tell her off but then she stopped, connected to her higher self, and asked the frantic woman, "What size are you looking for?"

The lady was surprised, yet answered, "36 B."

Carol reached into the bin and said, "Here's one!" and she handed the 36B to her. This immediately changed the energy and tone of the search amongst all of the women. Each began shouting out her size and as the shoppers found bras of that size, they handed them to the person. Thus they all started helping each other, laughing in the process, rather than fighting each other.

The best reprisal of competition is doing well and succeeding, but also helping others get out of competition by not resisting it, instead looking inward to your higher self and asking, "How can I teach this person to get out of competition?" or "What can I say that is non-threatening or perhaps even complimentary?"

At the psychic classes at Intuitive Insights, students learn a tool called "Body of Glass." This tool enables them to not resist the energy of competition and helps them to see what doorways are in the aura to allow for competition to enter. The "Body of Glass" tool is the art of non-resistance. If people are competing with you, try asking them a question about themselves.

Perhaps you are not certain of yourself and you allow other people's opinions to be more important than your own confidence. If so, you can release that uncertainty and close the doors on competition that hinders your spiritual growth.

Tapes and CDs Available from Intuitive Insights

Tapes ($12) and CDs ($15) present step-by-step processes & techniques in Vessa's own voice:

1. *The Seven Secrets of Attraction.* Whether you are in a relationship or not, this will revolutionize your energy. The best tape made to bring your attractive energy to optimum capacity. (60-minute tape or CD.)
2. *Spiritual Tools to End Depression.* A great tape about the spiritual cause of depression and what to do about it. (Cassette tape only at this time.)
3. *The Energy of Completing Relationships.* You've made the physical separation. Now take back your power & energy. (47-minute tape or CD.)
4. *Winning Court Cases w/ Spiritual Tools.* A 'must have' tape if you are going to court. You *can* change the energy on your courtcase outcome! (47-minute tape or CD.)
5. *Removing the Veil: Talking to the Other Side.* Step-by-step process to communicate with loved ones who have crossed over. (45-minute tape or CD.)
6. *Famous British & American Poetry.* 27 famous poems by Walt Whitman, Edgar Allen Poe, Emily Dickinson, Robert Louise Stevenson and others set to original music.

Three ways to order:

1. Call it in at 858-509-7582.
2. Mail a check to Vessa Rinehart c/o Intuitive Insights, 4305 Gesner Street, Suite 200, San Diego, CA 92117.
3. Via the website www.myintuition.net.

About the Author

At the age of six, Vessa began communicating telepathically with animals. In 1984, at the age of 19, while attending UC Berkeley, she entered a clairvoyant training program at an intuitive institute in Northern California, and was hired on as a staff member. For the next 14 years, she trained others to develop their own psychic abilities. In the spring of 1997, she appeared in video productions with renowned psychic Uri Geller and fire-walking instructor, Jon Cotton.

Vessa earned a Master's Degree in Management of Non-Profit Organizations, and has served as Treasurer for the Berkeley Area Interfaith Council. She is also an ordained minister and for many years was the pastor of a non-denominational Christian church.

Today, Vessa is the Director of Intuitive Insights—an organization dedicated to teaching people to develop their own intuition and clairvoyance—and hosts her own weekly television show: *The Intuitive Insight and Alternative Healing Show* in San Diego. She is also a popular guest on Los Angeles radio talk shows.

Vessa also presents Intuition Workshops and Healing Seminars in major cities across the country, including Atlanta, Boise, Philadelphia, and Seattle, and has authored numerous articles in New Age publications.

For more information, see the author's website:

www.MyIntuition.net.

www.ingramcontent.com/pod-product-compliance
Lightning Source LLC
LaVergne TN
LVHW090950080826
845145LV00003B/963

9781891962295